SELF-EMPOWERMENT

Sam R. Lloyd
and Tina Berthelot

A FIFTY-MINUTE™ SERIES BOOK

CRISP PUBLICATIONS, INC.
Menlo Park, California

SELF-EMPOWERMENT

Sam R. Lloyd
and Tina Berthelot

CREDITS:
Editor: **Kay Kepler**
Designer: **Carol Harris**
Typesetting: **ExecuStaff**
Cover Design: **Carol Harris**
Artwork: **Ralph Mapson**

Copyright © 1992 Crisp Publications, Inc.
Printed in the United States of America by Bawden Printing Company.

English language Crisp books are distributed worldwide. Our major international distributors include:

CANADA: Reid Publishing, Ltd., Box 69559—109 Thomas St., Oakville, Ontario Canada L6J 7R4. TEL: (416) 842-4428; FAX: (416) 842-9327

AUSTRALIA: Career Builders, P.O. Box 1051, Springwood, Brisbane, Queensland, Australia 4127. TEL: 841-1061, FAX: 841-1580

NEW ZEALAND: Career Builders, P.O. Box 571, Manurewa, Auckland, New Zealand. TEL: 266-5276, FAX: 266-4152

JAPAN: Phoenix Associates Co., Mizuho Bldg. 2-12-2, Kami Osaki, Shinagawa-Ku, Tokyo 141, Japan. TEL: 3-443-7231, FAX: 3-443-7640

Selected Crisp titles are also available in other languages. Contact International Rights Manager Suzanne Kelly at (415) 323-6100 for more information.

Library of Congress Catalog Card Number 91-76251
Lloyd, Sam R. and Berthelot, Tina
Self-Empowerment
ISBN 1-56052-128-7

This book is printed on recyclable paper with soy ink.

INTRODUCTION

The decision to write a book on self-empowerment was sparked by the strong interest that has developed in organizations about the idea of empowering others. The gurus of "excellence," "total quality" and "customer service" have trumpeted the message that empowering people is one of the key ingredients of success. We agree wholeheartedly with this prescription!

As training consultants, our interest in this area has helped us to understand the complexities of teaching people to empower others. Having worked with thousands of people in every kind and size of organization in ten countries has convinced us that only self-empowered people are good at empowering others! Those who struggle most with the idea of empowering others are individuals who lack something in their own sense of empowerment. People who are trusting, self-confident, positive in their outlook and effective in their relationships most naturally empower others.

As we developed this book we were also thinking of the need for each person to develop his or her own power and abilities to improve personal effectiveness and success. The self-empowered person has the best chance to accomplish goals, to make relationships work and to enjoy life to the fullest. Workers demonstrating competence, loyalty and a positive attitude are the most likely to be selected for empowerment by the manager.

Our idea of self-empowerment includes the common-sense awareness that anyone with high self-esteem, self-assurance, personal skills and competence and interpersonal skills has a greater chance of success.

In this book you will learn about your personal needs for self-empowerment, how to build self-esteem, how to deal with people more effectively and how to improve some important management skills. When you have completed this book, you will have a personal development plan tailored just for you.

We encourage you to complete each exercise, practice the recommended techniques and immediately start the process of self-empowerment. We can help you understand the whys and hows of self-empowerment, but only you can make it a reality. We wish you success!

Sam R. Lloyd

Tina Berthelot

CONTENTS

CONTENTS (continued)

S E C T I O N

1

The Need for Self-Empowerment

THE NEED FOR SELF-EMPOWERMENT

The need for self-empowerment has become even more obvious as companies have become aware of the importance of empowering employees. If an organization is to be successful, it must consistently achieve its goals, provide goods or services efficiently, keep up with or stay ahead of competitors, and satisfy those whom it serves (customers, patients, taxpayers, etc.). Truly excellent organizations accomplish all of this through the efforts of the people who make up the organization—but only when those people have the freedom to think and act, to question policies and procedures that interfere with quality or service, and to experiment and innovate.

We know that empowering people throughout the organization is a key element in creating excellence. To empower someone, you must give him or her the authority to make decisions and to act without having to get approval each time. It means allowing people to use their own intelligence, experience, intuition, and creativity to help the organization improve and succeed. Empowerment means keeping people informed and involved in the operations of the organization. It means listening to people and using their ideas.

The Question of Trust

It rather quickly becomes obvious that *empowering others requires trusting others.* Without trust in the abilities, intelligence, loyalty and motivation of others, a manager will have great difficulty with truly empowering them. A parent who lacks trust will be very reluctant to allow children the freedom to go where they want, when they want and with whom they choose.

WHAT IS YOUR TRUST LEVEL? SELF-EVALUATION

Evaluate yourself with the inventory below. Check each statement that you believe is true.

_____ 1. If you want something done right, do it yourself.

_____ 2. Most people enjoy personal achievements and want to do well.

_____ 3. When the cat is away, the mice will play.

_____ 4. I am comfortable letting people do things their own way.

_____ 5. I share my problems and feelings with at least a few people on a regular basis.

_____ 6. I worry when I don't know the status of projects.

_____ 7. You just can't get good workers anymore.

_____ 8. I prefer to receive frequent progress reports—daily would be ideal.

_____ 9. I want employees to tell me about problems as soon as they occur.

_____ 10. I frequently ask others for ideas about problems.

_____ 11. It's dangerous to confide in most people because they can't keep secrets.

_____ 12. A real leader makes decisions, gives clear directives, and does not tolerate anyone questioning his or her decisions.

If you checked only numbers 2, 4, 5, and 10, you display an unusual amount of trust in others. People who are trusting typically assume that others are honest and dependable. Trusting people are comfortable with sharing problems and feelings with others. People who trust others are people who see themselves as okay, and they see others as okay, too!

The other statements in the above list indicate some lack of trust in the abilities or motivations of others. Some are obvious while others are more subtle, but each reveals some distrust of other people. Whether the doubt is related to their dependability, commitment, skills, honesty, attitudes, motivation, or intelligence, the result is the same. When you do not trust, you will be very reluctant to empower others. You will also be afraid to confide in others or to allow them to be part of your efforts, which means that you miss opportunities to benefit from their support, assistance and creativity.

SELF-ESTEEM AND CONFIDENCE

An interesting aspect of trust is that people who have the highest self-esteem find it easiest to trust others. When a manager is confident in his or her own abilities, the fear of trusting others is diminished. When you have a high level of self-esteem, you are more likely to share problems or feelings with a friend or companion. On the other hand, if your self-esteem is fragile, you will worry about what others think of you and you will keep problems and feelings to yourself.

The self-empowered person finds it easier to trust because his or her self-esteem and confidence does not depend upon the approval of others. In the next section you will learn about the components of self-esteem and how to build your own self-esteem. One of the benefits of doing this is that you will increase your ability to trust and empower others.

The following case history illustrates the personal costs when business people lack self-esteem and self-confidence.

CASE HISTORY

Robert was an excellent student and athelete in college. Everyone expected him to have a successful career. By the time he was 30, those who had known him in his younger years were puzzled. Robert had changed employers three times since graduation, telling others that each move was part of his plan for moving up in the world of business.

His old acquaintances became aware that Robert seemed angry and stressed most of the time. He frequently complained about his boss and his employees. No one was surprised when he announced that he had been fired and was looking for another new job. Several months passed and Robert was unsuccessful in his job search.

In desperation, Robert applied for a position in a company where an old classmate, Paul, worked as personnel manager. Paul was surprised to see Robert's application because the position was lower in responsibility and salary than Robert's past employment. When he checked with previous employers, a pattern emerged. Each said positive things about Robert's decision making and motivation, but also suggested that he could use some help with his ability to deal with people.

During the interviews and assessment process, Paul noticed that Robert made disparaging remarks about his former employers and employees. For this reason, Paul chose another candidate—one who had a record of good relationships with people and who impressed everyone with his good communication skills.

CASE HISTORY EVALUATION

Which of the following characteristics did Robert seem to lack:

☐ Motivation?   ☐ Trust?

☐ Intelligence?   ☐ Enthusiasm?

☐ Experience?   ☐ Decision-making skills?

☐ Interpersonal skills?   ☐ Confidence?

Did you check trust as a missing characteristic? That might be a good guess, but there does not seem to be much evidence to indicate that was Robert's difficulty. If you checked interpersonal skills, you correctly identified his most obvious problem.

Robert's experience is a common one. Many talented people fail to achieve their potential because they do not have the skills for dealing with people. Research conducted by the American Management Association revealed that the typical manager spends as much as 80 percent of the workday in face-to-face interaction with other people. Interpersonal skills are necessary for success in almost every field or endeavor.

EFFECTS ON RELATIONSHIPS

Another important need for self-empowerment is to enable you to be effective in relationships with other people. Robert's experience illustrates one of the most common reasons for firing managers: they treat people with disrespect, and they are aggressive and abrasive. Organizations are most effective when people function cooperatively in teams that communicate well. Families are most successful when they share and support one another. Relationships of all kinds work best when each person has the skills and commitment to keep communication open and honest.

Who would you rather have as a boss? as a friend? as an employee? as a mate? the person described in list A or list B?

PERSON A	PERSON B
Someone who:	*Someone who:*
Passes along information to you	Keeps information to him- or herself
Asks about you	Limits conversation to impersonal topics
Listens well and often	Interrupts and does not listen
Seeks your opinion	Rejects your suggestions
Expresses appreciation	Takes you for granted
Shares concerns and problems	Keeps everything to him- or herself
Seems to care about you	Seems disinterested in you

Surely you selected A over B. Most people prefer to work with and live with others who are willing to expend some effort to make the relationship mutually rewarding and pleasant.

EFFECTS ON RELATIONSHIPS (continued)

Now turn the microscope around and examine yourself. Are you most like A or B in your relationships with your boss, your employees, your friends and your family? Think about each of those relationships separately. You may discover that you are guilty of making a half-hearted effort in at least some of your relationships.

Few people excel at all aspects of relationships, but self-empowered people do better than most!

The characteristics in list B are indicators that the person lacks some of the elements of self-empowerment. Hoarding information is a common means of control and self-protection, a strategy that often results from a lack of self-assurance. Restricting interactions to impersonal topics and avoiding self-disclosure may result from discomfort with intimacy or from a lack of trust. Anyone who becomes more self-empowered will improve their abilities for maintaining good relationships. Interpersonal effectiveness is easiest for self-empowered people.

PERSONAL SUCCESS

A final reason to develop self-empowerment is that it leads to personal success. How do you define success? Write a brief definition below.

Success is _____

_____

_____

_____

_____

_____

_____

_____

_____

_____

_____

_____

_____

Different people have differing ideas about success. Some think in terms of money, others in terms of accomplishments, and others in terms of love and happiness. We define success as *an ongoing process of setting goals and achieving them*. Success is a continuous experience and not some remote destination to be reached someday. It does not matter what your goals are (money, love, power, fame, etc.); when you achieve your goals you experience success.

An important part of being self-empowered is having clearly defined goals based on your own values, and on having the persistence and abilities to achieve your goals. Later in this book you will learn some valuable steps to help you define achievable goals as part of your personal development plan.

As you become more self-empowered you will have the tools and skills for creating more successes in your life. To start this process, turn to the next section to learn about building your self-esteem.

S E C T I O N

2

Building Self-Esteem

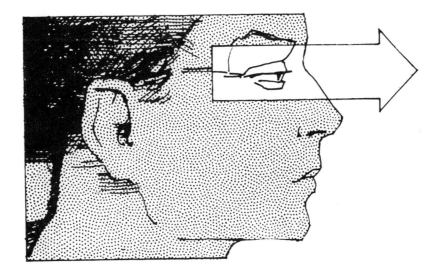

BUILDING SELF-ESTEEM

A self-empowered person is someone who has high self-esteem. It is difficult to imagine how someone without self-respect and self-confidence could ever be considered a self-empowered person. Building your self-esteem is a major factor in becoming self-empowered.

What is self-esteem? Find out if you agree with us by deciding which of the following statements are true or false. Circle T for true or F for false.

What Is Self-Esteem?

		True	False
1.	Self-esteem can vary depending upon situations, events, health, etc.	T	F
2.	Self-esteem is a blend of internal confidence and external achievements.	T	F
3.	Self-esteem is something anyone can increase and maintain at a higher level.	T	F
4.	Self-esteem is affected by early life experiences.	T	F
5.	The level of your self-esteem is reflected in your judgments of yourself.	T	F
6.	Our beliefs and values can make it difficult to maintain high self-esteem.	T	F

If you marked all of the items true, your understanding of self-esteem agrees with ours. Self-esteem varies in each of us and is shaped and affected by many factors.

To better understand how self-esteem is developed, we will break it down into three components: self-image, self-talk, and self-determination. When you understand how each of these separate factors operates and how to change each, you will be able to build your own self-esteem to a higher level. This may be the most important accomplishment for becoming a self-empowered person.

SELF-IMAGE

If we asked you, "What is your self-image?" you might have a difficult time putting into words how you see yourself. You probably do not have a day-to-day awareness of your self-image, but you do have one and it affects how you live your life every day. Your self-image affects how you interpret what people say and do, how you choose to act in a situation, and how you feel about yourself and others. It is a constant influence on your perceptions of yourself, others, and life in general.

CASE HISTORY

Virginia Jackson has been an employee of Michael's Farm Equipment Company for several years. During the past several months she has been part of a team providing support for the distributors who sell the company's products. This morning she was informed that she has been selected to head a new team to provide customer service support for the distributors. She will be allowed to select her own team members and she will have a reasonable budget to develop the services and systems for this project.

Virginia is surprised and pleased to receive this assignment. Later she talks with a friend about the new assignment and says, "You know, Susan, I'm really surprised that I was given this opportunity. I'm such a disorganized person that I never dreamed that management would even consider me for such an important job. The thing that really scares me the most is making the presentation to the management group about how we will approach the assignment. I just don't think I'm enough of an outgoing person to do something like that without looking foolish!"

CASE HISTORY EVALUATION

With this brief look into Virginia's life you can probably tell how she sees herself. What do you suspect she believes are her strengths and weaknesses?

Strengths	Weaknesses
_____	_____
_____	_____
_____	_____
_____	_____
_____	_____
_____	_____
_____	_____
_____	_____
_____	_____

With such a small amount of evidence we can only guess about Virginia's self-image, but she would seem to have some ambition and confidence because she was pleased to receive the assignment. She seems to be a trusting person because she is confiding in her friend Susan. Her weaknesses include seeing herself as a disorganized and shy person. She seems to expect that she will do something that will result in others seeing her as foolish.

YOUR OWN STRENGTHS & WEAKNESSES

SELF-IMAGE (continued)

Now that you have thought about Virginia and her self-image, take a few minutes to think about your own self-image. In the space below, list your strengths or positive characteristics and also list your weaknesses or negative characteristics.

Strengths	**Weaknesses**
_____	_____
_____	_____
_____	_____
_____	_____
_____	_____
_____	_____
_____	_____

Which did you find easiest to identify—your strengths or your weaknesses? Many people tend to be more aware of their faults than their positive qualities. If that is true for you, it will be important for you to learn to give yourself credit for your strengths and to break the habit of giving more weight to your weaknesses.

Did you list an equal number of strengths and weaknesses? We provided the same number of spaces for each, but you may have thought of more in one category than the other. If you listed more negative characteristics than positives, start paying more attention to your positive attributes and add some new strengths to your list as you work your way through this book and complete other self-improvement projects.

Another aspect of this inventory of your self-image is that some of the personal traits that you listed as weaknesses or negative characteristics can be evaluated differently if you change your perspective. For example, Virginia perceives herself as disorganized (which may be true), but others may be impressed with her enthusiasm and creativity. It is a common pattern that enthusiastic, creative people tend to be disorganized.

What you see as a fault or undesirable trait may be viewed by others as one of your endearing qualities. We often apply a negative label to ourselves, using an excessively harsh judgment that may be viewed more positively by a more objective observer. It is possible to look at ourselves from a different perspective by considering other ways to describe the same characteristic with more realistic or forgiving words. Examine the list below and write a more positive description of the same quality in the space provided.

Negative Trait	Positive Version
lazy	_____
shy	_____
loud	_____
fat	_____

Was that difficult? Did you figure out a way to describe each of the negative traits in a more forgiving, less negative manner? Here are some that we thought of for the list above. Lazy = laid back, minimalist, energy conserving. Shy = quiet, retiring, unobtrusive. Loud = enthusiastic, exuberant, vocal. Fat = large, robust, hefty.

Now return to your list of personal negative characteristics and do the same with your own negative self-judgments. Figure out a way to describe those traits with less severe, more accepting words.

We are not recommending that you engage in self-deception, but it is important to allow yourself to feel better about yourself by learning to be less critical of your traits. You may have some behaviors that need to be changed and we will address those later in this book.

SELF-TALK

Do you talk to yourself? ☐ YES ☐ NO

We hope that you answered yes, because everyone does! Self-talk is something that each of us does with some frequency. It is a normal practice, so don't be concerned about it. Some people do it aloud and some even have two-way conversations.

The big question to answer is: How do you talk with yourself? Do you say positive, supporting things to yourself, or do you berate yourself and say disapproving things? If you habitually say negative things to yourself, you are keeping your self-esteem at a lower level than it could be.

Just imagine how you would feel if you had a hypercritical boss looking over your shoulder every day telling you how badly you were doing and how you would never improve. Imagine what it would be like to have a disapproving parent with you at all times to chastise you any time you made a mistake, broke a rule, or forgot something.

That is exactly what many of us do to ourselves with negative self-talk throughout our lives. Some who have studied this aspect of human behavior have estimated that as much as 80 percent of the average person's self-talk is negative! It is easy to understand how that much daily disapproval could erode anyone's self-esteem.

Read the examples below and check any that are similar to things you have said to yourself.

☐ "I can't believe I missed my exit! Boy, am I stupid!"

☐ "I hope I don't forget what I'm supposed to say. I don't want to make a fool of myself."

☐ "I can't believe I just said that. I'm always putting my foot in my mouth!"

☐ "Slow, slow! I am so darned slow."

☐ "You did it again, dummy! Don't you ever learn?"

☐ "Oh no! I'm such a klutz!"

☐ "I just can't figure it out. I've never been any good at this."

Did they sound familiar? Almost everyone does this to themselves and it is important to acknowledge that you do. It is also important to become aware of how often you do this and what your most frequent self-denigrating remarks are. This is the first step toward changing this habit into a self-empowering technique.

SELF-TALK (continued)

Write below some of the negative self-talk you know you use with some regularity. Take your time and recall recent situations in which you failed to live up to your own expectations.

My Self-Criticism

_____

_____

_____

_____

_____

_____

_____

_____

_____

_____

_____

_____

_____

If you think of more as you proceed, turn back to this page and add them to this list. To help you remain aware of this habit, we suggest that you keep a journal for the next few weeks. Each day record some of your self-talk or keep a total of the negative and positive self-talk each day. Until you become aware of your self-talk, you will be unable to change it into supportive and encouraging messages.

Read some of the messages you identified with in our list on page 19 and some of the ones you wrote in the self-criticism exercise. Imagine saying those things to a valued employee or a friend or family member. You might think, "Heavens, I would never say that to them!" Isn't it interesting that we say such things to ourselves? You can learn to be as considerate of yourself as you are of others.

This is a particularly difficult aspect of building your self-esteem because many of the negative labels each of us gives ourselves were applied to us early in life by other people. As small children we heard adults saying that we were a certain way, and we believed them. Most grown-ups know that "little pitchers have big ears" but they do not know that they come equipped with tape recorders. Some of the disapproving messages we hear become part of our self-image and perceptions of reality.

Did you ever hear messages such as these? Check those that are close to what you heard.

- ☐ "You're such a rowdy child."

- ☐ "If you can't say something nice, don't say anything."

- ☐ "Don't you talk back to me!"

- ☐ "You're always knocking into things!"

- ☐ "Where did you ever get such a silly idea?"

- ☐ "You'll never have any friends if you act like that."

- ☐ "Don't you ever think before you speak?"

- ☐ "Good boys and girls don't do things like that."

Did you check at least a few? Most of us heard hundreds of such messages as we grew up and many of those became part of our own self-images. Adults often communicate judgments of a child's worth when they are responding to the child's behavior. Unfortunately, we hear that we are "bad" rather than that a behavior needs to change for our own benefit. It is also unfortunate that many children hear more negative judgments than positive ones, and the negative messages make a strong impact.

SELF-TALK (continued)

We're not trying to make you angry with the adults who were early influences in your life. Almost everyone has such experiences—they are a natural part of personality development. Your challenge now is to break free of the limits on your self-esteem that may have resulted from such early lessons. Everyone carries a load of early labels and self-defeating habits. Becoming self-empowered means lightening that load.

Here are some load-lightening guidelines. When you hear yourself saying (internally or aloud) things such as the expressions in the left-hand list, learn to say instead something like the kinder examples in the right-hand list.

Old Self-Talk	New Self-Talk
"I'm so clumsy!"	"Oops, I spilled my coffee."
"Boy, that was stupid."	"I wasn't paying attention—stay alert."
"What if they don't like my idea?"	"This is a good idea—I hope they like it."
"I can't go on that trip until I get caught up at work."	"I want to go, and the break from work will do me good."
"I should visit my parents."	"I could visit my parents and it's okay to go skiing if I want."
"I'll never get the hang of this."	"Calm down, think clearly—you can do it."

It may take some practice to learn to change your self-talk from restricting your self-empowerment to allowing it. By sticking with your commitment, keeping a journal of negative self-talk, and practicing saying more positive and energizing things to yourself, you will experience an exciting new feeling of power!

SELF-DETERMINATION

A final part of building self-esteem is to become more self-determined. What does self-determination mean? Read the following case history to understand it.

CASE HISTORY

JACK'S LAMENT

Jack is a sales manager who is within six months of retirement from his lifelong employement in sales. We hear him talking with a peer over lunch. "It's hard to believe that I'll be retiring in another six months." His friend asks, "Are you looking forward to it, Jack?"

"You bet I am! Maybe now I'll have some time to do things I've always wanted to do. I've enjoyed my work but it demanded so much of my time and energy that I never seemed to find time to travel or do a lot of other things. I mean, Fran and I have had a good life but so many things seemed to pass us by. We intended to do more fun things but just never seemed to be able to find the time. Maybe now we can."

The friend comments, "Well, you'll certainly have the time now!" To which Jack responds, "Yeah, but I'm not sure that my retirement income will be enough for us to afford much beyond the basics. Inflation has been so bad that we're not going to be as comfortable as I had hoped."

Jack is an example of the many people who go through life allowing events and others to determine how they live life. To such people, life seems to be happening to them rather than something that they determine for themselves. These people often look back and wonder where all the time has gone and how they managed to get so little pleasure from their lives.

Self-empowered people approach life differently. They are goal-directed individuals who have a clear understanding of what they want from life and go about making sure that they get it! Obviously, such a person needs high self-esteem and positive expectations to accomplish their goals. They need to see themselves as someone who deserves what they want and who is capable of achieving whatever they set out to do.

In reality, everyone's life is self-determined. Those who are passive in their approach to life, reacting to events and allowing others to set their priorities, are responsible for choosing to live their lives passively. When you are self-determined, you actively identify your own values, wants and needs, define your own goals, and chart your own path through life.

A SELF-CHECK QUIZ

Rate yourself on the following items. Circle 1 if you are weak in that area, 3 if you are average, and 5 if you are strong. Be honest with yourself.

	Weak				Strong
I set specific goals at least annually.	1	2	3	4	5
I have clear five-year goals and retirement goals.	1	2	3	4	5
I discuss my values and wants with family or friends.	1	2	3	4	5
I use a daily planner or ''to-do'' list.	1	2	3	4	5
I plan my leisure time to make sure I enjoy it.	1	2	3	4	5
I enjoy my work and get real satisfaction from it.	1	2	3	4	5
I feel like I am in charge of my life.	1	2	3	4	5
I accomplish most of my goals.	1	2	3	4	5
I manage money well and am saving for retirement.	1	2	3	4	5
I feel very satisfied with how my life is going.	1	2	3	4	5
I have successful personal relationships.	1	2	3	4	5
I have a good balance of work, play and family.	1	2	3	4	5

Now total your score.

If you scored in the 45–60 range, you are doing a very good job of determining your life. If your score is 25–44, you are among the great majority who manage fairly well but could get more satisfaction from life by improving your self-determination. If your score is 12–24, you have been letting life happen to you, and you will benefit greatly from completing the rest of this book and mastering the ideas and techniques.

Regardless of your score on this quiz, you will benefit from increasing your self-empowerment. Being self-empowered helps you to be more successful and satisfied in every aspect of your life. You will learn more about clarifying your values and setting goals in the section devoted to designing your personal development program.

S E C T I O N

3

Expectations and Outcomes

EXPECTATIONS AND OUTCOMES

One of the fascinating aspects of self-empowerment is the role played by a person's expectations and attitudes. When you contemplate a new challenge, do you expect an easy victory or a struggle? When you think about the party you will attend, do you anticipate having fun or being bored? Are you aware that your expectations have a powerful impact on your actual experience?

CASE HISTORY

THE THREE COWORKERS

Terry, Pat and Connie work in the same company and all are supervisors. Their performance is being scrutinized carefully by upper management as they decide who is the best candidate for promotion to middle management.

Terry is known as a hard worker who often comes early and stays late. Terry speaks frequently about having to work hard and shows signs of worry and stress. When the output of Terry's department is examined, the productivity is comparable to the other departments. The management team is surprised to discover that several employees have complained about the pressure in this department.

Pat has been with the company longer than the others and has been passed over before when promotion was considered. Pat's reputation is hampered by a persistent pessimism. Others joke about his stock reactions, which are "That will never work," and "If it ain't broke, don't fix it." Pat's department has the highest turnover and the lowest productivity.

Connie is a relaxed, efficient person who rarely comes early or stays late. Connie spends a lot of time moving about her department talking with employees. There are no grievances in her file and her productivity and turnover figures are the best of the three. The management team is impressed with how Connie gets so much accomplished without seeming to work hard at all.

CASE HISTORY EVALUATION

Do you agree that Connie seems to be the best candidate? ☐ YES ☐ NO

If Connie is the star of this trio, what are her most important differences?

_____

_____

You might assume that Connie is a better delegator. You might also guess that her employees appreciate her for showing interest in them and for being readily available. Another insight might be how her relaxed, non-stressed style helps the employees feel less pressure. All of those things are probably true.

Why? _____

_____

Comparing Management Styles

Connie
The key factor in Connie's more effective management style is her underlying expectations and attitudes. She seems to expect others to be responsible and dependable. She has positive expectations about life in general, which allows her to be relaxed and free of stress. Her frequent contact with employees indicates that she genuinely likes people.

Terry
In contrast, Terry expects things to be difficult and believes that success requires hard work. Terry seems to sweat and strain unnecessarily, causing others around her to feel "pressure."

Pat
Pat's most obvious characteristic is a negative attitude. Pat responds spontaneously by seeing only the faults and reasons for not being cooperative. You can imagine how Pat's face must look and the tone of voice he uses when he makes these negative remarks. No wonder people leave this department!

POSITIVE ATTITUDES PRODUCE POSITIVE BEHAVIOR

Each of these people display different behavior and it is the behavior that influences others. Each person's behavior is a consequence of underlying expectations and attitudes. If Pat and Terry decided to change their outlooks, their behaviors would also change.

The phenomenon known as a self-fulfilling prophecy explains this whole process. People see what they expect to see, experience what they expect to experience, achieve what they expect to achieve, and fail when they expect to fail! The famous entrepreneur Henry Ford once said,

> *If you think you can or you think you cannot, you are always right!*

The Subconscious

Mr. Ford understood that we unconsciously program ourselves to experience life just the way we assumed it would be. Part of this phenomenon is "selective perception." We constantly filter out most of the sights and sounds around us, allowing only a manageable amount through to our conscious awareness. This is necessary for our sanity. The perceptions that we allow ourselves to be aware of are those that are consistent with our expectations and attitudes.

For example, have you ever purchased a new car? Do you remember how you suddenly started noticing all of the cars on the road that were like the one you bought? Those cars were there all along, but you only noticed them when you changed your expectations and awareness.

The subconscious mind is a powerful influence on our perceptions and our behavior. Subconscious expectations and attitudes result in your noticing some things and not others, being sensitive to some words and not others, and saying and doing some things and not others. It is a constant process.

Self-empowered people take charge of this process and program themselves to have positive experiences in life. The self-empowered person has expectations and attitudes that result in success by prompting effective behavior and by influencing others in positive ways.

WHAT DO YOU EXPECT?

Respond as spontaneously and honestly as you can to each of these situations. What would you expect in each case?

1. Your boss tells you that you will be making an important presentation to the senior management group in two days. What is your reaction? What is your mental picture?

_____

_____

_____

_____

2. Your spouse asks you to accompany him or her to a reunion of his or her high school graduating class and you agree to go. What are your expectations?

_____

_____

_____

_____

3. You are hired to be the manager who supervises the three people described in the previous case history: Terry, Pat and Connie. What are your expectations for each relationship?

Terry _____

Pat _____

Connie _____

In each case, if your answer represents your genuine expectation, your actual experience would be very likely to turn out just as you expected. If you respond to your boss's surprise assignment with pride and pleasure and you expect to do well, you probably will. If you react with dismay or anger and expect to have difficulties, you probably will.

If all you can imagine about accompanying your spouse to the reunion is being bored or uncomfortable with so many strangers, then you will have just the experience you expect.

The third situation is very common. If you have some advance information about someone, that information will prejudice your perception of that person and help to create just what you expected to happen in your relationship. Most people would expect to feel tense with Terry and would probably plan to counsel him or her about time management. Most would expect conflict with Pat and an ongoing struggle to obtain cooperation. And most of us would predict a smooth, successful relationship with Connie.

Sure enough, the relationships proceed just as expected!

Self-fulfilling prophecies are a powerful influence in our lives. The challenge is to become aware of our deep-set attitudes and expectations and change those that are self-defeating. This includes expectations of others as well as ourselves.

To help you become more aware of some of your expectations and attitudes, complete the self-evaluation exercise on the following page. As usual, be as honest as you can when answering.

SELF-EVALUATION

WHAT ARE YOUR PREJUDICES? SELF-EVALUATION

Write an A in the blank if you agree, or D if you disagree.

_____ 1. Most people want to do their best and achieve good results.

_____ 2. Men are better decision makers than women.

_____ 3. Most organizations exploit people when possible.

_____ 4. Some people do as little as they can get away with.

_____ 5. Young people today don't appreciate the value of money.

_____ 6. Women are better suited for parenting than men.

_____ 7. You don't tamper with success.

_____ 8. Most people care only about themselves.

_____ 9. If you want something done right, do it yourself.

_____ 10. People with college degrees make better managers.

Did we hit a nerve or two? Did you allow yourself to answer honestly? It is difficult to admit to some of our own prejudices, but we all have them and it is important to recognize them.

What are the correct answers? There is research to substantiate some of the above statements and to repudiate others, but the "right" answer is not that important for this exercise. *The important point is that whatever you believe about each one is what will influence your perception and actual behavior in situations related to that issue!*

If you believe that men are better decision makers than women you will tend to discount the thinking of women (regardless of your own sex) and to give more credit to men's ideas. If you expect people to work hard and do well, they probably will; but if you expect them to give minimum effort, they probably will. Your expectations get communicated through subtle daily behaviors, and people usually respond the way you thought they would!

DRAMATIC DEMONSTRATIONS

In a carefully designed experimental study, researchers chose at random 20 percent of the students in an elementary school and told the teachers that they had unusual potential for intellectual growth. The names were selected by using a random number table, which means that they were determined by the ''luck of the draw,'' not by any actual testing. Eight months later these children were tested; the ''gifted'' ones had made significantly higher gains in intelligence scores than the other students. Because the teachers expected them to do better, they did!*

Proof of the self-fulfilling prophecy phenomenon in the world of organizations was evident as long ago as 1890. The U.S. Census Bureau installed new tabulating machines that required census workers to learn new skills that were thought to be difficult. The workers were told that after some practice they would be able to punch about 550 cards per day and that processing more than that number might be harmful to their psychological health. As you might expect, after two weeks they were processing a little over 500 cards per day and reporting stress symptoms when they exceeded that number.

Additional clerks were hired later to operate the same machines, but were told nothing about limits on the productivity rate. After only three days, the new workers were processing over 2,000 cards per day with no ill effects. The original workers *believed* that they could produce only 550 cards and that is what they did. The new workers had *no limiting expectations* and produced at a much higher rate.*

* R. Rosenthal and L. Jacobson, *Pygmalion in the Classroom* (New York: Holt, Reinhart and Winston, 1968).

SELF-FULFILLING PROPHECY

The power of self-fulfilling prophecy is almost frightening when you consider these examples, but it is also very exciting when you think about how much we can each accomplish when we choose to start with positive expectations. It is also exciting to consider what a positive influence each of us can be for the other people in our lives when we have positive expectations for them!

To put self-fulfilling prophecy to work in a self-empowered way, you must learn to truly believe in the ''win–win'' or ''I'm okay—You're okay'' philosophy. When you have genuine positive expectations and attitudes about yourself, you will experience much more success. When you have positive expectations of others, you act as an influence on them and help each of them be more successful, too.

IDENTIFICATION QUIZ

Put a check mark by the situations below that are okay–okay or win–win examples.

_____ 1. A manager says to an employee, ''I'm impressed with the thoroughness of this report, Tracy. I can always depend on you to do a good job!''

_____ 2. When a team member arrives late for a meeting, the leader rolls his eyes up and exhales loudly.

_____ 3. A parent speaking to a teenage child says, ''Don't forget to clean your room today and don't leave your dirty clothes piled up in the corner this time.''

_____ 4. A teacher speaking to a student says, ''You are going to learn a lot about how nature works in this section.''

_____ 5. Two managers are talking about their teams. One says, ''Even though the people on my team are mostly new, I can tell that they are going to set some records.''

_____ 6. An employee asks the manager, ''Will you check this and give me some feedback?''

_____ 7. One worker says to another, ''Isn't that typical? You can always count on management to make things more difficult!''

_____ 8. An employee notices another struggling with a complaining customer over the telephone and offers a smile and a ''thumbs up'' hand signal.

_____ 9. A friend compliments you on your presentation, saying, ''That was a super job. I could never pull that off so smoothly.''

_____ 10. A manager is thinking about conducting a performance review with an employee: ''I don't know how to handle this one. This is going to be really tough for him to take.''

CHECK YOUR ANSWERS

IDENTIFICATION QUIZ ANSWERS

The authors picked numbers 1, 4, 5, 6, and 8 as win–win examples. Numbers 2, 3, 7, 9 and 10 communicate negative expectations and numbers 9 and 10 reveal self-defeating expectations.

A final suggestion to help you become more self-empowered by putting the power of self-fulfilling prophecy to work is to encourage you to use the idea of "self-programming." To develop the habit of assuming positive outcomes in your life, practice by writing statements such as these on index cards or self-adhesive notes:

I can learn to dance the tango.

I can ask my boss for a raise.

I can confront Bob about his late arrivals.

In preparation for actually doing these things, read the messages to yourself several times each day for a week or two before you take the planned action. Your chances for success are greatly improved by "programming" your expectations for positive outcomes.

Joel Weldon, a professional speaker, has said,

Success comes in cans, not in cannots!

We agree!*

---

* For more information on self-programming, order *Developing Positive Assertiveness* by Sam Lloyd and/or *Stress That Motivates: Self-Talk Secrets For Success* by Dru Scott using the information in the back of this book.

S E C T I O N

4

Interpersonal Skills

INTERPERSONAL SKILLS

The self-empowered person has high self-esteem, a positive self-image, and positive expectations and attitudes—all of which help to assure success. We all live and work in a world full of other people, and another important aspect of being self-empowered is having skills for interacting effectively with these people. Even the most positive and confident person will not accomplish much without the skills to communicate and cooperate with others. Here are some examples of situations in which the ability to communicate effectively is important.

What to Do?

1. Sandra works in the finance department. She has the training and the experience to qualify for a supervisory position that has opened up in her department. Sandra enjoys her current work, but lately she has been aware that she no longer feels challenged. She would like to earn more money and is seriously thinking about telling her boss that she would like to be considered for the supervisory position. Sandra is hesitating because she is not sure whether she wants the additional responsibility or if she would enjoy supervising others.

What steps do you recommend for Sandra? _____

_____

_____

2. Martin has been working on a project that is a new challenge for him; it requires creativity and some new ways of thinking. Marsha, who has handled similar projects, has dropped by a couple of times to offer helpful suggestions. Today she pauses before leaving Martin's office and says, ''Martin, I'm never sure whether you appreciate my help or not. I can't tell what you really want.'' Marsha leaves with a friendly wave.

Martin wonders about her comment and realizes that he is not sure about his preferences. Marsha's suggestions have been useful and have helped him progress more quickly, but he is aware that he might feel better about his accomplishment if he did it without her help.

What do you think Martin needs to do? _____

_____

_____

WHAT TO DO? (continued)

Did you recommend that Sandra do something to help her decide what she really wants for herself? That would be a necessary first step before she can decide what other actions to take. Did you suggest that Martin needs to do the same thing? His friend has noticed that he is sending mixed signals, and he himself is wondering about what he really wants.

It may seem simple to us when we examine another person's situation, but knowing what you want when it is your own life is not always so easy. Until someone knows what they want, they often are stymied about what to do or say. Learning to identify your own "want" in a situation may take some practice and it is a good starting point for improving your interpersonal skills. Practice identifying your "wants" in the following examples.

SITUATION	I WANT
Your boss gives you a complicated assignment that must be completed by 5:00 tomorrow.	
Relatives arrive for a surprise visit expecting to stay a week.	
You were planning to eat alone and read a good book when two coworkers ask you to join them.	
Your spouse asks if you would like to join his/her after-work gathering of coworkers or meet at home later.	
You win a contest and have a choice of $200 or a "mystery prize" guaranteed to be worth at least $200.	

Did one or more of the situations require a little thinking before you could decide? Did you discover that you had more than one want in a situation? For example, you might want advance notice from your boss or more time for completing the assignment. You might want to spend time with your relatives, but you might want them to check with you before coming for a visit. You might want to read your book, but you might want to chat with your coworkers or make sure that you are considered to be a friendly person.

Most of our life situations present us with options, and making choices can prove to be challenging. The self-empowered person has an awareness of his or her own values and preferences, and feels comfortable with allowing his or her wants to be the most important deciding factor rather than what might please others.

Often it is easier to decide what you do *not* want. That can be a helpful first step toward identifying your wants, but it is important to become aware of what you *do* want. Knowing only what you do not want can lead to being passive in your dealings with others. Knowing what you do want and actively assuring that you get your wants satisfied is a necessary part of being self-empowered.

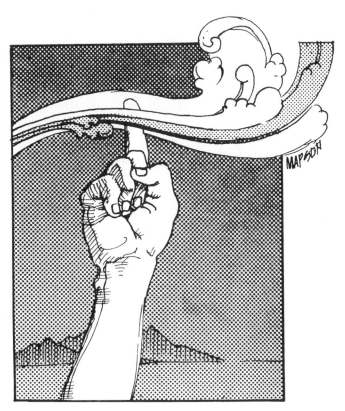

SAY IT STRAIGHT

Our friend and fellow training professional, Abe Wagner, is fond of saying, "Say it straight or you'll show it crooked!" His observation is accurate. Knowing what you want is not enough to be effective with other people. To have any chance to have a situation turn out the way you want it to when others are involved, you must also know how to communicate directly and clearly.

Which of the following are "straight" communications that clearly convey what is wanted; which are vague and unclear? Beside each communication write the letter C for clear or V for vague.

_____ 1. You wouldn't want to go to the movies tonight, would you?

_____ 2. Why didn't you let us know you were coming?

_____ 3. Will you please proofread this sometime today?

_____ 4. You know, maybe we should postpone this until later.

_____ 5. Please schedule a meeting with Fred and Mary to discuss the budget sometime next week.

_____ 6. Are you sure you want to go camping this weekend?

_____ 7. I would prefer to have more information about these new locations before making a commitment on the proposal.

_____ 8. I want to be considered as a candidate for the position in Finance. Do I need to complete an application?

_____ 9. Do you think you might be able to approve a raise for me in the next budget?

_____ 10. I don't enjoy violence in movies. Will you recommend another movie or consider playing miniature golf instead?

If you marked numbers 3, 5, 7, 8 and 10 as clear communication, you agree with the authors. To help you understand why the others are not clear, we offer the following explanations.

In number 1, the person speaking seems to want to go to the movies, but instead asks the other if they *don't* want to go. It is a passive, negative approach to getting a want satisfied. Number 2 comes across as an attack, asking the other to explain their behavior rather than communicating what the speaker wants. Number 4 is tentative and passive, which allows others to make the decision. Number 6 asks whether the other person is firm in their desire rather than stating what the speaker wants. Number 9 is passive and tentative which makes it easy for the other person to say no.

GUIDELINES FOR CLEAR COMMUNICATION

To communicate clearly what you want, use "I-statements."

Examples:	"I want to visit the tropical rain forest someday."

"I feel like doing something fun tonight."

"I would appreciate your asking me before telling other people that I will participate."

Practice:	Write I-statements to communicate your want in the following situations.

Relatives arrive for an unannounced visit.

_____

_____

Your boss gives you a complex assignment with only 24 hours to complete it.

_____

_____

When you need the cooperation of others to get what you want, it helps to use a clear directive or straightforward request. We recommend using the "magic question": "Will you please?" Other requests such as "Do you think you might?" "Can you?" "Could you?" or "Why don't you?" are more tentative and passive and are less likely to get cooperation.

Examples:	"Please read this and tell me what you think about it."

"Will you please approve a raise for me in the next budget?"

Practice:	Write a directive (command) that instructs someone to prepare a report for you.

_____

_____

Write a request asking someone to do something with you.

_____

_____

Most of what we accomplish in life requires the cooperation and support of other people. Clear communication helps to get this cooperation, but does not guarantee it. To improve your chances for getting willing cooperation and real commitment from others, we suggest using a contractual approach for dealing with others. This requires a two-way communication or negotiation that results in a clear understanding of who will do what and when.

CASE HISTORY

Marge is very frustrated because the sales representatives in her region do not consistently get their biweekly reports to her on time. She is talking about this with Tom, a fellow office employee: "I don't know how I am going to get those sales reps to cooperate! I have told them again and again that they need to have their reports to me by the deadline, and half of them just ignore me!" Tom asks, "Is it always the same ones who are late?" Marge answers, "A couple of them are almost always late, but each report period some of the others miss the deadline, too. I never know which ones it will be, but I don't think I have ever had all of them on time!"

CASE HISTORY EVALUATION

Does Marge have a clear understanding with each of the sales representatives about their reports? _____

Has Marge asked for a clear commitment? _____

What do you recommend that Marge do to improve the situation?

_____

_____

_____

_____

_____

_____

_____

_____

If you said no to the first two questions, you agree with the authors. We recommend that Marge use I-statements and a clear request with each representative to get a better understanding and commitment. She could say something such as, "I need to have your sales report by Wednesday each time to give me enough time to prepare the summary report for the regional manager. Will you please help me by making sure you get your report to me by then?"

Marge telling the representatives that "they need to do this" was not communicating her own wants and needs in a direct way. Her communication style sounds parental and may prompt resentment or rebellion rather than cooperation.

If you suggested that Marge have her boss intercede, that would probably get results. The sales representatives might feel resentful that she took that approach and she will not gain the respect that being more self-empowered and negotiating her own agreements would earn.

To better understand what we mean by using a contractual approach, consider what a contract is. It is an agreement between two or more people in which each promises something to the other. To make certain that the agreement will be honored, it is a good idea to structure the contract to meet the basic requirements of a valid contract.

Contract Guidelines

1. **Each party clearly states wants/needs and each clearly agrees.**

Each asks, "Will you please . . .?"
Each responds, "Yes, I will."

2. **Each person benefits from the agreement.**

If only one person gains, the other or others may feel victimized later and break their promise.

When each person benefits, everyone has some motivation to keep the agreement.

3. **Each person can do what they promise.**

Each must have the ability and resources to do what they promise. This guideline is often broken when people make unrealistic time commitments.

4. **The agreement must be legal.**

If the contract violates a law or established policy or rules, it is an unenforceable contract. To avoid disappointment and conflict, make sure that agreements stay within the rules.

SAMPLE CONTRACTS

A CONTRACT AT WORK

Bill is in charge of a project to develop some new product concepts and marketing projections. He and his team have decided that, to do a good job, they need more time and some additional funding. They need to use a consulting firm for some marketing research data, and they need time to evaluate different consultant proposals. Bill is planning to approach his boss, Joan, to negotiate for the time and money. Help Bill prepare by completing the following:

What can Bill offer to Joan as a benefit for her?

_____

_____

_____

_____

_____

Write an I-statement and a request for Bill to use when asking Joan for what he wants.

_____

_____

_____

_____

_____

Authors' ideas: Bill could offer a higher-quality finished project using the marketing research data. He could say, ''My team and I believe that we could improve our projections with some marketing research data and we need more time and some additional money for a consulting firm. Will you please approve an extension of three weeks and an additional $3,000?''

A CONTRACT BETWEEN FRIENDS

Virginia and Sue work in the women's clothing department of a retail business. They are good friends. Sue has an opportunity to attend a social hour with a new male friend and to go with him to a concert after dinner. She is excited about the evening and hopes to convince Virginia to close out her cash register and prepare her daily report so that she can leave right at closing time to prepare for this special date. Help Sue with her negotiation by completing the following:

What can Sue offer Virginia as a benefit?

_____

_____

_____

_____

_____

Write an I-statement and a request for Sue to use.

_____

_____

_____

_____

_____

Authors' ideas: Sue could offer to do the same for Virginia on another occasion. She could say, "Virginia, I have a date with a great new guy I met. He is taking me to a social hour, dinner, and a terrific concert, and I would like to leave right at quitting time to get ready. Will you please close out for me, and I'll do the same for you another time?"

UNDERSTANDING CONFLICT

An important reason to approach dealing with other people in this contractual manner is to prevent conflict. When people do not have clear and fair agreements, conflict often results. Preventing such situations is a major reward of using the win–win philosophy and open, honest negotiation.

Not all conflict can be prevented, and resolving conflict can be one of the most difficult tests for the self-empowered person. A valuable explanation for how conflict happens was developed by psychiatrist Stephen Karpman.* He recognized that conflict involves people playing predictable roles with one another, and he represents these roles as a triangle arrangement.

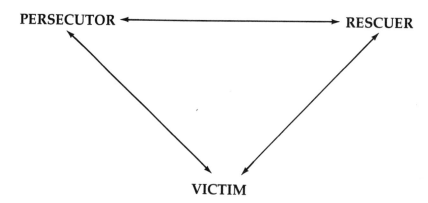

Identify each of these roles in the following conflict situations.

THE DOCTOR'S OFFICE

Mr. Cannon has been waiting about 30 minutes to see his doctor when another patient who arrived after him is called into the examining room by a nurse. Mr. Cannon charges to the receptionist's desk and says loudly, "What's going on here? I've been wasting my time out here for half an hour and now you're letting someone in to see the doctor before me! I demand that you get me in there right now!"

The receptionist replies, "Oh, I'm so sorry. I don't know how this has happened, but I can't leave the desk unattended and I'm sure the doctor will see you soon if you'll just wait a little longer." Mr. Cannon roars, "If I don't get to see the doctor right now I'm going to get a new doctor and I'll make sure your boss knows you were the cause!"

*Stephen Karpman "Fairy Tales and Script Drama Analysis," Transactional Analysis Bulletin VII, No. 26 (April 1968), pp. 39–43.

The office manager, Mrs. Ratchet, walks up and says, ''Mr. Cannon, I apologize for this mix-up, and I will instruct the nurse to take you right into examining room B and let the doctor know that you have been waiting quite some time. I'm sure he will get to you as soon as possible.''

Who is playing the role of PERSECUTOR? _____

Who is playing the role of VICTIM? _____

Who is playing the role of RESCUER? _____

THE COPY CENTER

Beverly has just received 85 copies of the handout materials she will use for a presentation to all of her company's regional and district managers and top executives. She discovers that two pages are missing entirely and that other pages contain several errors. She is dismayed to see that none of the illustrations were printed in color as she instructed. She runs to the copy center.

''You idiots have ruined my presentation! I know I can't expect much from this joke of a department, but this is the worst screw-up yet and I'm going to make sure the president hears about this one!'' Jack, the copy center manager, responds, ''What right do you have to come down here yelling at us? You always bring your stuff in at the last minute and expect us to work miracles for you! If you want perfect work, you'd better get your act together and allow some realistic lead time, lady!''

Who is playing the role of PERSECUTOR? _____

Who is playing the role of VICTIM? _____

Who is playing the role of RESCUER? _____

UNDERSTANDING CONFLICT (continued)

THE DIFFICULT ASSIGNMENT

Kelly is struggling with how to present some figures as part of an important report that is due soon. After seeing Kelly wad up page after page and throw them into the wastebasket and hearing several deep sighs of frustration, Stacy walks over and says, "Why don't you show them that information in a pie chart? Being able to see all of those figures in a visual form should help make the relationships of the figures more obvious."

Kelly responds, "Why couldn't I think of that? I never can figure out anything that involves so many numbers!"

Who is playing the role of PERSECUTOR? _____

Who is playing the role of VICTIM? _____

Who is playing the role of RESCUER? _____

Answers:

In the doctor's office scene, Mr. Cannon is the PERSECUTOR, the receptionist is the VICTIM, and the office manager, Mrs. Ratchet, is the RESCUER.

In the copy center situation, Beverly first feels like a VICTIM and then becomes a PERSECUTOR. Jack probably feels like the VICTIM of Beverly's attack and retaliates by playing PERSECUTOR. The role of RESCUER was not involved.

In the difficult assignment case, Kelly is acting like a VICTIM with repeated sighs and histrionics and Stacy plays the role of RESCUER. There was no PERSECUTOR.

We are sure that you were able to recognize the roles and that you are probably aware of how familiar such situations are. Each of us experiences thousands of brief situations such as these during our lives. It is important to learn to recognize our own roles in such cases, because *all three roles are undesirable ways to deal with other people!*

To help you understand the truth of this last statement, we will examine each of these three situations to explain how each role has undesirable consequences.

In the doctor's office, Mr. Cannon's persecutory behavior communicates disrespect for the receptionist, which is an ''I'm okay–You're not okay'' or win–lose approach. If he gets his way with this kind of behavior, he is likely to use the same approach again and again, alienating people and setting himself up for retaliation. The self-empowered person gets his or her wants and needs met with win–win approaches rather than intimidation.

What could Mr. Cannon have said if he were self-empowered?

_____

_____

The receptionist behaved as a VICTIM by cowering under Mr. Cannon's attack and acting helpless about what to do. The self-empowered person does not allow the behavior of others to prevent clear thinking and feeling okay about oneself.

What could the receptionist have said to demonstrate self-empowerment?

_____

_____

Mrs. Ratchet's role is the most subtly inappropriate, because the role of RESCUER appears to be desirable at first glance. When one person steps in uninvited to rescue another, that action communicates a lack of respect for the ''victim.'' Rescuing someone reinforces their being helpless rather than helping them become self-empowered. There is also a good chance that the RESCUER will later feel like a VICTIM because they did all of the work.

If Mrs. Ratchet were self-empowered, she would allow the receptionist to handle the situation and would become involved only upon request. She would also provide training for the receptionist to help her develop skills for dealing with irate customers (thus empowering the employee).

UNDERSTANDING CONFLICT (continued)

In the copy center case, Beverly took her VICTIM feelings and turned them into a PERSECUTOR attack on Jack, which invites retaliation and continuing resentment. It will also result in a loss of respect from everyone who hears about it.

What would a self-empowered Beverly have said?

_____

_____

Jack reacted just like Beverly, allowing her words to trigger bad feelings and a retaliatory attack. His response will further strain their working relationship and make it more difficult for them to resolve the situation in a win–win manner.

What would a self-empowered Jack have said?

_____

_____

In the difficult assignment case, Kelly feels helpless and sends out subtle VICTIM messages, hoping a RESCUER is in the vicinity. This is like announcing, "I'm not okay–You're okay," which is not a self-empowered win–win approach. Kelly may get help in this passive manner, but at the cost of others perceiving her as less capable than themselves.

What would a self-empowered Kelly have said to get help?

_____

_____

Stacy steps in to RESCUE Kelly with a good suggestion, but probably feels less respectful of Kelly (at least at a subconscious level) and may resent Kelly's not doing her own work. The rescue also reinforces Kelly's feelings of inferiority about numbers and does not help her learn to ask for assistance in a self-empowered manner. Stacy could have demonstrated self-empowerment by acknowledging Kelly's frustration and asking whether Kelly would like some suggestions. Even more empowering for Kelly would be if Stacy knew how to use probing questions to prompt Kelly to think of her own solutions to the problem.

The more consistently you interact with others in a self-empowered manner, the fewer conflict situations you will help to create. You will never be able to control the words, actions or feelings of others, so you will continue to find yourself having to deal with others who are playing Persecutor, Rescuer, and Victim. The bad news is that you will be unable to completely stop playing the three conflict roles. Everyone learns to play these roles early in life and we never seem to give them up entirely. However, reducing your frequency of participation in conflict with others by even a small percentage will feel wonderful, and you will gain respect from others!

THE SELF-EMPOWERED LISTENER

In many interactions with others the most important interpersonal skill is listening. No matter how skillfully one person chooses and delivers the words, communication does not occur if the other person does not listen. Self-empowered people know that good listening skills demonstrate respect for others and improve the odds for successful win–win interactions.

A Listening Quiz

What would you say if you were the listener in each of these examples? Write your response in the space provided.

1. "I think I'll quit this crummy job! Management doesn't even know I exist and only college graduates ever get promoted here."

_____

_____

2. "Mommy! Daddy! Billy said he doesn't like me anymore and he won't ever play with me again!"

_____

_____

3. "Look what you made me do! Why are you always sneaking around looking over my shoulder?"

_____

_____

4. "Why do we have to have all of these meetings? Most of them are a waste of time and boring to boot!"

_____

_____

5. "Please arrange a conference with the media department to discuss the new campaign. Be sure to check with the client about the deadline date and prepare a summary of the progress reports for everyone who will be in the meeting."

_____

_____

THE ROLE OF LISTENING

Before we deal with your listening responses, we want to establish what the role of listening is in communication. Ideally, a listener provides a response that will prove to the speaker that he or she has been heard and understood. In addition, the ideal response confirms for the listener that what was heard was understood accurately.

Most people go through their entire lives without receiving any actual instruction or training about how to listen. We all assume that because we have ears we know how to listen. Because we haven't been taught how to listen, most of us have learned by copying the listening behaviors of others, and we listen just the way everyone else does. Most of our own listening responses are quite predictable.

Some of our habitual listening responses do not confirm that we have heard correctly and do not provide any proof to ourselves that our understanding is correct. Worse than that, some of our habitual listening responses create communication roadblocks or lead to conflict situations. To illustrate, consider your responses to the five listening situations in the listening quiz.

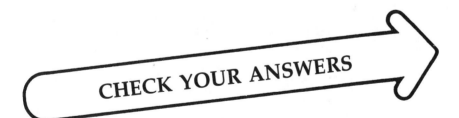

CHECK YOUR ANSWERS

LISTENING QUIZ RESPONSES

► **Situation 1:**

Many people respond to this situation by asking specific questions, offering advice, or saying something encouraging. If you used one of these responses, write the type in the space, or label your response if it is something other than these three.

_____

► **Situation 2:**

Most parents say something reassuring or explain that Billy will change his mind after he has calmed down. Write down which one you used, or label your response if it is different than one of these two.

_____

► **Situation 3:**

Many people respond with an apology, attempt to logically explain their actions, or say something critical about the speaker's behavior. Write down which you used, or label your response if it is different than these three.

_____

► **Situation 4:**

Some people agree with these remarks, while others will explain why the meetings are necessary, say something humorous, or attempt to calm the speaker with reassurances. Write down which of these you used, or label your response if it is different.

_____

► **Situation 5:**

Most people will say okay or "Yes, sir," or "Yes, ma'am." Some might ask a question and a few might even make a sarcastic remark such as, "Yes, your royal highness!" Write down which you used or label your response if it is different than these.

_____

If your listening responses were different than the ones we said were most likely, we will ask you soon to do some thinking about your responses. Now let us consider how the most frequently used responses fail to meet the test for an ideal response and how they might actually create communication problems.

PITFALLS OF THE POPULAR RESPONSES

ASKING QUESTIONS

When the listener starts asking specific questions, the speaker will usually answer, which often results in the listener unintentionally directing the communication away from what the speaker wanted to share or think about. A common form of question is the "closed question," which can be answered "yes" or "no." These questions tend to shut down communication.

OFFERING ADVICE

One undesirable outcome of offering advice can occur when the person acts on the advice and it proves to be bad advice. They will return to PERSECUTE. Another pitfall of giving advice is that the speaker may reject every offered suggestion, which results in both people feeling frustrated. A final undesirable outcome occurs when the speaker acts on the advice and it proves to be good advice—they will be back for more!

SYMPATHY or REASSURANCE

A serious pitfall of this well-intended response is that the speaker may interpret it as insincere or patronizing. Even if it is accepted as genuine, another risk is that the person will become dependent upon this support and will continue to seek it by playing a VICTIM looking for a RESCUER.

LOGICAL EXPLANATION

This response is used frequently when the speaker has said something critical of the listener. However, rational explanations usually accomplish little, because the speaker is operating in an emotional or judgmental mode and hears the rationale as making excuses.

APOLOGY

Apologizing is almost an automatic response when someone accuses the listener, but it can sound like VICTIM, which only encourages the PERSECUTOR player to continue the attack. It is appropriate to apologize when you have behaved inappropriately.

PITFALLS OF THE POPULAR RESPONSES
(continued)

RETALIATION

Saying something critical or sarcastic to the speaker is another common reaction when the listener feels attacked or taken advantage of. All it will accomplish is to fan the flames of conflict.

HUMOR

Humor can be a valuable way to defuse an emotional situation, but frequently the listener's attempt at humor will be heard as a criticism or as an indication that their situation is not taken seriously by the listener. This will lead to conflict.

AGREE

If the listener agrees with the opinions or position of the speaker, that person may decide to do something foolish because they hear that they are "right." Later they will blame the listener for encouraging them. In situation 5, if the listener agrees to the directions by saying "Okay," or "Yes, sir," or "Yes, ma'am," the risk is that part of the instructions were misunderstood and an unnecessary mistake occurs.

A Word of Encouragement

This may be valuable. We are not telling you that these popular listening responses are always wrong. There is often no adverse effect when you respond in these ways. However, any time you use one of these responses you take a risk that you will end up in a conflict situation that could have been avoided if you had used a different listening approach. We will explain how to respond differently before concluding this section.

If you used any listening responses other than the ones we predicted, please write the label for each of those in the spaces below. Next, think about how each of those responses might in any way result in undesirable outcomes in the communication situation. You may want to ask another person to contribute their ideas about the possible pitfalls associated with your responses.

Your response _____

Possible pitfalls _____

_____

_____

_____

_____

Your response _____

Possible pitfalls _____

_____

_____

_____

_____

Your response _____

Possible pitfalls _____

_____

_____

_____

_____

LISTENING WITH LESS RISK

Some listening responses have a much lower probability of adding to or creating conflict. You probably already use some of them. Becoming more aware of your responses is a step in the direction of self-empowerment.

▶ Attentiveness Signals

You demonstrate attentiveness by making good eye contact, nodding occasionally, looking interested with facial expressions and body postures. The occasional "Uh-huh," "I see," "I hear you," and so on also communicate attentiveness. These signals create the impression that you are listening *but they prove nothing about whether you have understood a single word.*

▶ Prompting Signals

To encourage the speaker to open up or elaborate, you can tell or ask them to by saying, "Tell me more," "Please continue," "Go on," or "Then what happened?" "What more would you like me to know?" or "What are your thoughts on that?" These are "open" directives or questions that allow the speaker to say whatever he or she wants to communicate. They do not have the pitfalls of the "closed" or specific question. *These signals do not prove that you have heard a word correctly!*

▶ Verbal Restatement

To prove that you heard and understood correctly, restate what you think the speaker just said to you. We recommend using the following formula for a restatement that will prove both *empathy* and *understanding.*

- *Paraphrase content.* Restate an abbreviated or reworded version of the information or thoughts communicated by the speaker. This will prove that you did understand.

- *Acknowledge feelings.* Listen to the voice and interpret other body language signals to detect what feelings the speaker may be experiencing (most people won't say) and verbally acknowledge these feelings. This will prove that you have empathy.

- *A check-out question.* End your restatement with a brief "check-out" question such as "Right?" or "Did I hear you correctly?" This allows the speaker to respond to your feedback and will keep the communication flowing.

Examples:

Craig says to Sally, ''Oh no! I forgot to submit my expenses yesterday! Now it will be another month before I get reimbursed!''

Sally responds, ''Gosh, Craig, you sound worried about having to wait so long for your reimbursement, right?''

Craig answers, ''You bet I am! I need that money now!''

Notice that Sally proved she had understood accurately and she also demonstrated empathy by acknowledging Craig's concern. Craig knows he has been heard by someone who cares and Sally knows that she heard correctly. Sally also has avoided playing RESCUER.

Jim says to Dan, ''Boy, Dan, you've really put me in a bind. I needed that information today to complete my report. My boss is going to kill me!''

Dan replies, ''You seem disappointed that I don't have the information for you, Jim. Is that right?''

Jim responds, ''No, Dan. I'm angry! You've got me in real trouble.''

Notice that Dan was inaccurate about Jim's feelings and Jim immediately corrected him. Dan was correct with the content feedback and the communication continued. Now Dan can acknowledge Jim's anger and concern about being in trouble, which will help them resolve this situation with a win–win outcome.

PRACTICE YOUR VERBAL RESTATEMENTS

LISTENING WITH LESS RISK (continued)

Practice

Write in the missing portions of the verbal restatements for the examples below.

1. "Here comes Mrs. Green! She always complains about our music and about not having enough selections in her size!"

   "You seem _____ about having to deal with

   Mrs. Green's _____, right?"

2. "Dadgum it! I've added this three times and I get a different answer every time!"

   "Sounds like you're _____ with _____

   _____. Am I on target?"

3. "You never think of anyone but yourself! Why don't you ever ask what I would like to do?"

   "I hear that you think _____

   and you sound pretty _____. Is that right?"

Author's responses:

1. fed up, frustrated, or annoyed; Mrs. Green's complaints
2. frustrated; your report, all those numbers
3. I'm selfish, I don't ask you what you want; hurt, angry

SOME LISTENING TIPS

▶ Avoid using the same opening phrase with your feedback. After the third time you say, ''I hear you saying . . . ,'' your responses will sound insincere or mechanical.

▶ Watch out for exaggerating or minimizing the other person's emotional level.

▶ Concentrate on what the person is actually saying and do not attempt to guess about what they are not saying. You don't want to come across as a psychoanalyst!

▶ If the other person notices that you are restating and responds defensively, simply explain that you are only attempting to make sure that you are understanding correctly. Most people will be quite accepting of your restating when they understand its purpose.

One of the important uses of the restatement technique is helping to resolve conflict situations. As we stated, everyone becomes involved in conflict. It is simply too easy to blunder into the roles of PERSECUTOR, RESCUER, and VICTIM no matter how hard we work at staying out of them.

When you are faced with someone playing any one of the three roles of conflict, use the three-part feedback formula with them. This has the effect of lowering their emotional level, while preventing you from stepping into one of the conflict roles. When people feel empathy and understanding, they will more quickly step out of a conflict role and communicate with you in a more reasonable and rational manner.

Your self-empowered skill of active listening helps keep you out of conflict and helps other people join you in a win–win negotiation process. Everyone benefits, which is the whole idea of being self-empowered and using the win–win philosophy!

SOME LISTENING TIPS (continued)

In this section we have offered some suggestions about how you can improve your interpersonal skills as part of your program to develop self-empowerment. The self-empowered person is not only effective in getting what he or she wants, but also does so in a manner that empowers others by communicating respect and facilitating win–win outcomes.

In the next section we will help you improve some important management skills that will allow you to be more self-empowered in supervising others. These skills are equally valuable in personal relationships.

S E C T I O N

5

Improving
Management Skills

IMPROVING MANAGEMENT SKILLS

If you are in a management or supervisory position, it is critically important to be a self-empowered person. It is much easier for the self-empowered person to handle the responsibilities of management and the stress that accompanies management of people. Without self-empowerment, the role of manager can be a constant stream of anxiety-producing moments.

The most challenging aspect of management is the constant process of dealing with the most complicated creatures on earth—human beings. In the previous section you learned some valuable things about dealing with people, and in this section we will focus on improving your skills with people in some specific management situations that often prove difficult for most people.

By developing more skill in several important supervisory functions, you will be building your self-confidence and competency and this will add to your growing self-empowerment. Only the self-empowered manager is really any good at empowering others. When you become a skilled manager, everyone will benefit—you, your employees, and your organization.

WHAT ARE YOUR MANAGEMENT SKILLS? SELF-EVALUATION

Rate yourself between 1 and 5 on each of the management skills listed below, using 1 = weak, 3 = acceptable, and 5 = excellent.

1. Setting goals and priorities.	1 2 3 4 5
2. Keeping employees informed.	1 2 3 4 5
3. Delegating responsibility to employees.	1 2 3 4 5
4. Solving problems and making decisions.	1 2 3 4 5
5. Coaching employees when they make mistakes.	1 2 3 4 5
6. Giving positive recognition.	1 2 3 4 5
7. Seeking input and ideas from employees.	1 2 3 4 5
8. Confronting problem behavior.	1 2 3 4 5
9. Giving meaningful performance evaluations.	1 2 3 4 5
10. Using your time efficiently.	1 2 3 4 5

How did you do? Did you recognize some management skills that could use some improvement? Few managers are excellent in all of the skills listed above, so if you rated yourself as less than 4 or 5 on some of them, you have a lot of company!

If you have the courage to do it, we recommend that you ask each employee to rate you on these same skills to find out how they perceive you as a manager. You might learn that you are not as good at some of these things as you think you are.

In our experience with thousands of managers, we have found that several of the skills listed above predictably produce lower scores for most managers. We will concentrate on these skills in this section and suggest other sources to help you with the other ones.

PERSONAL INTERACTION

The skills that managers are most frequently weak in have a common characteristic—they are the ones that require face-to-face interaction with employees. Many managers are good at planning, making decisions, solving problems, and using time efficiently, but few are truly skillful at interacting with the people they manage.

CASE HISTORY

MARVIN THE MANAGER

Marvin asks Tony and Ellen to join him in his office. He says to Tony, "The monthly production figures are too hard to use, and it's taking too much of my time to analyze all this stuff. Take this report and summarize each section for me. Also break out the comparison figures for the improvement over last year for each team. I'll want you to do this for me each month, Tony, okay?" Tony responds, "Uh, sure. I'll get right on it."

Marvin turns to Ellen and says, "Ellen, I've been getting lots of complaints from the shop supervisors that the support staff is uncooperative. They're going to have to understand that their job is to provide assistance to everyone in this organization and that includes the shop supervisors. I need you to get that across to them." He looks expectantly at Ellen who answers, "I'll talk to them in the staff meeting Monday, but I know they are going to complain that the shop supervisors don't give them enough time to . . ." Marvin interrupts Ellen and says, "I don't want to hear their excuses. I want you to make sure they start doing a better job! That's all. You both can get back to work now."

CASE HISTORY EVALUATION

How do you rate Marvin's delegation skills? _____
Check each item below that you think he needs to improve on and compare
your answers with the authors'.

☐ Instructions are specific and clear.

☐ The employee is given enough authority to do the job.

☐ The manager confirms that the employee understood accurately.

☐ The employee is given authority to make decisions and suggestions.

☐ Responsibility rather than a specific task is delegated.

☐ The employee receives encouragement and positive expectations.

☐ A system for follow-up evaluation is established.

☐ The employee is encouraged to ask clarifying questions.

Authors' evaluation:

We checked all but the first category for Marvin. His instructions are
specific and clear, but he could improve on all other counts.

Marvin is guilty of a very common management mistake. He doesn't
seem to understand the difference between delegating and dumping! By
assigning specific and somewhat menial tasks to Tony each month, he is
ignoring the opportunity to redesign the whole reporting system, which
could provide a one-time solution for his problem. He has dumped a
boring, routine task on an employee when he could have delegated a
challenging responsibility.

Marvin repeats his mistake with Ellen by dumping the undesirable task of lecturing the support staff rather than investigating the problem to discover the root causes. Ellen attempted to suggest that there were other aspects to be considered, but she was interrupted by her manager, who apparently assumes that his answers are the only right ones.

You can imagine the conversation between Tony and Ellen after they left Marvin's office. Do you think that their respect for their manager may have dropped a notch or two? How do you think they feel about their assignments?

The self-empowered manager knows that delegation is a complex skill that requires preparation and good communication skills. The self-empowered manager knows that delegation is an important tool for empowering employees and adding to their job satisfaction and self-esteem.

THE ART OF DELEGATION

WHY IS DELEGATION SO DIFFICULT?

List as many reasons as you can to explain why so many people find delegation difficult to do well.

_____

_____

_____

_____

We have asked many managers to do this in training programs and here are the most common answers we have received.

1. **Lack of trust.** Too many people still seem to believe the old saying—''If you want something done right, do it yourself.''

2. **It takes longer to delegate than to do it myself.** This is often a rationalization and the actual time difference is negligible. Even when the statement is true, the manager will probably have to do this same task again and again; investing a little more time to delegate today saves a lot of time in the future.

3. **I enjoy doing it myself.** This is a common reason for holding on to jobs that could be delegated. Good managers know that they must look beyond their own preferences and consider what is best for accomplishing goals, for the entire organization, for the development of employees, and so on.

4. **I don't have anyone with experience or skills.** This is a good reason for being reluctant to delegate, but the solution is obvious—provide some training.

5. **I'm afraid they might do it better than I can.** This is scary if you are not self-empowered! Smart managers understand that you can't be better at everything than your empoyees are, and you will impress people more by knowing how to use the strengths of your team.

There are many reasons why managers of all levels fail to delegate skillfully. One of the things you must accomplish to be a self-empowered manager is to recognize that, regardless of your reasons, one of the keys to being a successful manager is knowing when and how to delegate.

PREPARING TO DELEGATE

To help you improve your delegation skills, we recommend that you answer the following questions before each delegation.

1. **What is the goal or objective of delegating this task?**

By answering this question you will identify the expected outcome of the delegation. This will help you to delegate a responsibility for outcome rather than a meaningless task.

Example: Marvin could have defined his delegation goal as redesigning the production reports to produce information that could be used without so much additional analysis.

Practice: Define the delegation goal for the problem that was given to Ellen in the earlier example.

---

2. **Who will I select for this assignment?**

This question requires you to consider your candidates. Who is the most qualified? Who would most like to do this? Who needs the growth experience? Who has the time? Who could handle this with some training?

Example: Marvin might have selected Tony because he is familiar with the production process, likes working with numbers, and has a good relationship with the production team.

Practice: What factors might Marvin have considered in choosing Ellen for the other delegation?

---

3. **What kind of authority or power is needed and how much is required?**

This answer is important if the person is to be empowered enough to be successful. Assigning a responsibility without giving appropriate power will almost always guarantee failure.

Example: Marvin would need to give Tony authority to ask the production people for different data, to experiment with different formats, and possibly to call upon people in other departments such as accounting, quality assurance and data processing for assistance.

Practice: What authority would Ellen need for her assignment?

PREPARING TO DELEGATE (continued)

4. Who else needs to know about this delegation?

Your employee only has authority when others know that you have given this power. Think about all who may be involved in the process of carrying out this delegation and be sure that each one is informed about it.

Example: To assure Tony's success, Marvin would need to inform the production crew, accounting, quality assurance and data processing that he has authority to request their help with the project.

Practice: Who would need to know about Ellen's assignment and the extent of her authority?

5. What type of control or feedback will I need?

A major concern about delegating is the loss of control, so you need to figure out how you can reduce this stress factor. What kind of information will you want about progress and how often? Do you need some type of safeguard to catch costly errors in judgment? How will you meet your need for control so that you avoid looking over your employee's shoulder (which communicates distrust)?

Example: Marvin might want Tony to discuss new format designs with him before implementing them. He might want a weekly progress report.

Practice: What controls or feedback would Marvin want in Ellen's case?

6. What is a reasonable time limit for completion?

You may want to involve the delegatee in answering this question. A clear deadline helps to focus efforts and increases the probability of success. The time limit needs to be realistic for both your needs and your employee's.

Example: For Tony's assignment, a reasonable time limit might be several months or longer to allow for experimentation with different reporting formats and for developing the computer programming. It could take longer, depending on the amount of data needed and the complexity of the redesign challenge.

Practice: What would be a reasonable time limit for Ellen's assignment of resolving the conflict between the shop supervisors and the support staff?

7. **When and how will we evaluate the performance?**

Planning for evaluation in advance assures that you will identify the measures of success and arrange some system for providing the information that will be needed for evaluation. The delegatee deserves positive reinforcement of a good performance and coaching assistance with any problems.

Example: Marvin and Tony will need to evaluate how well the new reporting system provides the needed data. They also will want to evaluate how Tony went about resolving the problem. The evaluation might include asking others who were involved to evaluate Tony's role.

Practice: What aspects of Ellen's performance will need to be evaluated and how might it be done?

_____

_____

It is very important to plan for delegation in order to be sure that the assignment will be completed successfully. Delegation is an important opportunity to strengthen your relationship with the delegatee and to empower him or her so that everyone benefits.

Communication

The next major step in delegation is to communicate with the person selected for the assignment. Here are some guidelines to assist you with this important communication challenge:

- *Meet face-to-face without time pressure.* Written communication is more easily misunderstood than verbal give and take. Allow time for questions and to discuss alternatives. It is a good idea to put a summary of the agreements in writing after the meeting.

- *Ask rather than command.* The great majority of people prefer to be asked rather than told what to do. This subtle demonstration of respect is important.

- *Check for understanding and commitment.* Don't ask "Do you understand?" or "Okay?" because most people will say yes even when they don't clearly understand. Ask the delegatee to summarize what you have discussed. Also be sure you received a definite commitment; don't accept "I'll try," because this answer signals a potential failure.

- *Agree on the control procedures and the follow-up date.* If you and the employee agree about how you will be kept informed, you will not need to check up on him or her. If you both know in advance when and how the performance will be evaluated, the delegation is more likely to be successful.

- *Inform others about the delegation.* Your delegation is not complete until you have told everyone who may be affected or involved.

CASE HISTORY

MARVIN'S SECOND CHANCE

Marvin asks Tony to join him in his office. ''Tony, I'm having trouble using the production figures. I have to spend too much time analyzing the data. I know that you are familiar with the production process and that you are good with numbers. You also have a solid relationship with the production people, so I would like for you to figure out a better way to report this information. Are you willing to take this on?''

Tony responds, ''I would love to! What are the biggest problems with the way the information is reported now?''

Marvin answers, ''I can't tell at a glance how each team is doing with respect to production goals or in comparison to the other teams. I also have to spend a lot of time looking up last year's performance figures to check our improvement.''

Tony says, ''Okay, that gives me a better idea of what you need. May I get some help from Sherry in data processing? She is our best programmer and I'll bet she'll have some good ideas about how to get this data reported in more useful ways.''

Marvin answers, ''Sure, Tony, and I'll authorize whatever computer time you two will need. I'll also tell all of the production people that you are going to need their cooperation. Anything else?'' Tony says, ''Not right now, but I may have more questions later.'' Marvin ends with, ''Ask anytime, Tony. Will you give me a weekly progress report and present your ideas to me before we make any changes in the system?'' ''Sure, boss.''

CASE HISTORY EVALUATION

Quite an improvement, right? Even though this still is not a *perfect* delegation, it is a good one. Few of us ever achieve perfection, but excellence does not require perfection. Tony and Marvin will have a better relationship. Tony will do a better job with this assignment, and the improvement in efficiency will be many times greater than the original approach. Marvin has also grown a little in his self-empowerment by having empowered Tony!

A Practice Challenge

Write down your ideas about how to delegate the other assignment to Ellen and practice with a friend or family member.

_____

_____

_____

_____

_____

_____

_____

_____

_____

_____

_____

_____

_____

_____

REFINE YOUR DELEGATION SKILLS

Like any other skill, delegation is developed with practice. Knowing what to do is not enough by itself!*

CASE HISTORY

A BIG MISTAKE

Tony and Sherry have responded enthusiastically to their challenge and have generated many ideas about how to improve the production reporting. They have designed a new form for the supervisors to use in reporting the information to data processing, so that they will have what they need for a newly designed report to Marvin. Predictably, the supervisors are resistant to having to change and they have complained to the production manager. The production manager tells Marvin, "Tony has my supervisors in an uproar, Marvin. They are complaining to me about all of these new forms and they don't understand why we're always changing things!"

Marvin encounters Tony in the hallway talking with Sherry and two other employees and says angrily, "Tony, I told you not to change any forms until you had cleared your ideas with me! You've got everyone in production mad. Not only have you not helped me with my problem— you've created a bigger one!"

---

* For more help with improving your delegation skills order *Delegating for Results* by Robert Maddux from the list in the back of this book.

CASE HISTORY EVALUATION

A familiar scene? Tony has made a mistake but Marvin has made an even bigger one, hasn't he? What is Marvin's first mistake?

_____

_____

If you said his mistake was confronting Tony in front of his peers, you agree with the authors. An important factor in handling the mistakes of others is to choose an appropriate time and place.

Recall some of your own mistakes and check each of the items below that were unpleasant for you.

- ☐ Feeling self-disgust

- ☐ Angry about wasted time

- ☐ Fear of discovery

- ☐ Feeling embarrassed

- ☐ Rebuke by boss, parent, etc.

- ☐ Teasing by friends, peers

- ☐ Public reprimand

- ☐ Asked to explain why you did what you did

- ☐ Lack of coaching help

- ☐ Punishment of some type

You may have checked several of the choices because different mistake situations produce different outcomes and each person reacts differently to each response. Now reconsider all that you checked and decide which one or two are the ones you most dislike and circle those. Do you think others might react the same?

HOW TO TREAT MISTAKES

One of the most predictable situations in organizations of all sizes and all types is how mistakes are handled. It is very common for most managers and most organizational systems to have some type of disapproving or punitive response.

When mistakes result in angry lectures, suspension or probation, reductions in income, written documentation of poor performance, or even termination of employment (all common responses), an unwritten rule is being communicated to employees. This ''rule'' is the unspoken expectation that employees will make *no mistakes!* Is this realistic? _____

Of course not, but this perception exists in most organizations and work groups. When this is the unwritten expectation, how do employees approach their work? _____

If you said cautiously or fearfully, you are aware of the problem of treating mistakes harshly. Yet, time and again, employees receive only punitive responses to their mistakes. No wonder so many resist change and efforts to find ways to improve. They know that changing things increases the probability of making mistakes, and they are not going to take that chance if they don't have to. Why set yourself up for punishment?

Possibly the biggest price that organizations pay for treating mistakes with punitive responses is the lesson that employees learn about how to handle their own mistakes. What do many learn to do about having made a mistake?

_____

Everyone knows the answer to this last question—cover it up! Why do managers continue to handle mistakes so badly when the cost to themselves and the organization is so obvious? We have concluded that the simple answer is that no one has ever taught them how to do it any better! All of our lives we have been criticized by parents, teachers, and our own bosses for making mistakes. When and how were we supposed to learn a positive, helpful way to treat the mistakes of others?

The self-empowered manager knows that mistakes are *opportunities for improvement*. When employees make mistakes, it is an opportunity for the manager to coach them through a process to identify the cause of the mistake, identify corrective actions, and learn how to prevent the reoccurence of the same mistake. The following checklist will help you learn the self-empowered approach to handling the mistakes of others.

Self-Empowered Coaching

1. Demonstrate respect, care and reassurance.

The employee already feels bad about making a mistake. Say or do nothing to communicate disapproval and show that you care. "Everybody makes mistakes." "Don't punish yourself." "You just proved you're human."

2. Share one of your own mistakes.

Tell the employee about one of your own mistakes to help them feel better and to build trust in your relationship. People are less likely to hide mistakes from you when they know about some of your mistakes.

3. Ask one question and listen.

Ask an open-ended question such as "What happened?" or "How did this happen?" Keep quiet and allow time for the other to answer. If the employee is going to learn from this mistake, he or she must do most of the thinking. By telling you how the mistake occurred, they will be more likely to remember what was done incorrectly. Do not ask a series of fact-finding questions because you will be doing all of the thinking.

4. Ask another question and listen.

When the employee has identified what was done incorrectly, you ask "How can you fix it?" Again, it is important for the other person to do the thinking. When someone thinks of a solution, they are much more likely to remember it and follow through with it than if you thought of it for them. If they don't know how, work together to identify some possible alternatives.

5. Ask a final question and listen.

To help make sure that the same mistake will not be repeated, ask "How can you make sure this won't happen again?" Allow time for an answer, listen, and restate. It is important for the employee to figure out the actions needed to prevent reoccurrence; this increases the probability that they will learn from this experience.

CASE HISTORY

MARVIN TRIES AGAIN

Marvin learns from the production manager that Tony has designed new forms for the supervisors to report production results and that they are unhappy about all of the changes. He finds Tony in the hallway talking with Sherry and two other coworkers. He says, "Tony, when you finish here, will you check with me in my office?"

"Sure, Marvin. We just finished and I want to tell you about what Sherry and I have done, anyway."

When Tony and Marvin return to Marvin's office, Marvin says, "Before you tell me about your project, let me share something with you. Franklin was just in here telling me about your new forms and how the supervisors are resisting the changes. I'm unhappy about this because I thought we agreed you would clear any new forms with me before implementing them. Was that our agreement?"

"Uh, yeah, I guess I got excited about our ideas and forgot to check it out with you. I'm sorry."

"That's okay, Tony. We all make mistakes. I remember that my first week on the job here I got so excited about the project that I did some work that was only supposed to be done by someone with security clearance, and I had the security team all over me!"

"You're kidding!"

"Nope. I really did it. So you're telling me that in your excitement you just forgot to clear your ideas with me and I can understand that. How can you get the supervisors to calm down and work with you on this?"

"I think it would be a good idea for me to tell them that I jumped the gun a little and apologize for not communicating with you and them about our ideas before presenting them with a new form."

Marvin responds, "That might do it, Tony. I'll help you out with this by meeting with all of you to provide moral support. About all I will say is that you are helping me to figure out ways to make our reporting more useful." (Pause) "How can you make sure something like this won't happen again?" Tony answers, "I think it would be a good idea for me to meet with you each week to discuss our progress rather than submitting a written report like I was doing." Marvin says, "Good idea. Let's do it."

CASE HISTORY EVALUATION

Obviously, this approach takes a few more minutes than scolding Tony in the hallway, but the outcome is well worth the extra time and effort. Tony will have increased respect for Marvin because he handled the stiuation so skillfully and also because he revealed a little of his own imperfections. Marvin has added to his self-empowerment by turning a problem into an improvement in his relationship with Tony, and there is now a greater likelihood that Tony's project will have a successful conclusion.*

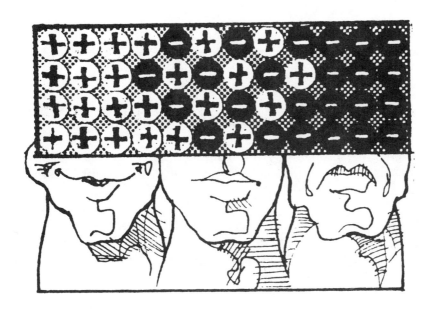

---

* For additional ideas about improving your coaching skills as part of your self-empowerment growth, we recommend that you order *Coaching and Counseling* by Marianne Minor from the list in the back of this book.

PEOPLE PROBLEMS

Problems with people are possibly the management situation that is most challenging and that requires the highest degree of self-empowerment. In this section we hope to help you build self-empowerment by sharing some valuable ideas about how to resolve such problems.

Think of one or more situations in which someone has been a source of problems for you. Choose one that has been frustrating or difficult for you to resolve, then complete the following items. Describe the problem that you have had with the other person.

_____

_____

_____

_____

_____

_____

_____

Now look back at your description and answer the following questions.

Did you describe the problem by referring to the person with negative adjectives (labels) such as "lazy," "uninterested," "arrogant," "stupid," etc.?   _____

Did you describe the problem in terms of the other's personality characteristics, attitudes or motivational level, such as "has a bad attitude," "doesn't care," "has an insulting manner," "does as little as he or she can get away with," etc.?   _____

When you think about the problem, do you find yourself thinking that the other person is the problem?   _____

Most people have to answer "yes" to the above questions, because most of us have learned to define the problem as the other person—we literally think they *are* the problem. That's the reason such problems have been called "people problems." The most commonly heard complaints from managers are that an employee has a "bad attitude" or is "just not motivated."

When problems with others are defined in these ways, the probability of a successful win–win resolution is extremely small. Why? Answer the following questions.

Can you change another person's personality? _____

Can you change another's lifelong attitudes and values? _____

Can you change another's motivational needs? _____

If you answered "no" to the last three questions, you agree with the authors.

Personality, Attitudes, and Motivational Needs

Personality is developed during the early years of childhood and most experts in the fields of psychology and psychiatry agree that personality does not change once it's formed. Even with extensive psychotherapy, people do not change their basic personalities. These core characteristics are like the foundation of a house, which we can build on as we go through life, adding rooms or remodeling, but the foundation remains untouched.

Attitudes reflect our core beliefs and values. Attitudes can change when a person's underlying beliefs and values change, but this rarely happens. It happens only when the person decides to change, and not when someone else attempts to change them. Change is most often prompted by some traumatic life event such as divorce, a major illness or accident, the death of a loved one, or losing a job.

Motivation has been studied for decades by many experts such as management professors and industrial psychologists. One of the basic things we know about motivation from all of this research is that motivation is a process of attempting to satisfy unsatisfied needs. A satisfied need does not produce motivated behavior. Offering you a banana split in an attempt to motivate you will be ineffective if you have just completed a large meal and are feeling stuffed.

Some motivational needs are basic and predictable: the need to survive, to be safe from harm, to have enough to eat and drink, and so on. Other needs are unique to the individual and are much less predictable. It is generally not possible to change someone else's motivational needs. About all anyone can do is to know someone well enough to understand his or her motivational needs and then provide whatever will satisfy those needs in the hope of getting some motivated behavior.

CHANGING PEOPLE'S BEHAVIOR

Well, if we can't change someone's personality, attitudes, or motivational needs, how can we hope to resolve people problems? Fortunately, the answer is quite simple: define the problem correctly. "People Problem" is an unfortunate misnomer—the problem is not the person. The problem is the person's *behavior*.

To resolve someone's behavior problem, you must be willing to confront them about the behavior and negotiate with them for a change. People can change behaviors much more easily than they can their personality characteristics, and it is actually the behavior that is the problem.

What is your reaction to the idea of confrontation? What do you imagine when you think about confronting someone? Check any of the responses below that fit with your expectations about confrontation.

_____ The other person will get angry.

_____ I will feel nervous.

_____ The other person will make excuses.

_____ I will get angry.

_____ The other person will cry.

_____ The other person will resent me.

_____ The other person will dislike me.

_____ It will hurt the relationship.

_____ It won't accomplish anything.

_____ The other person will counterattack.

_____ The other person will think I'm petty.

_____ Everyone will gossip.

Most people have had only negative experiences with confrontation, so they have negative expectations about confronting others. When you have been confronted by others in the past, it was probably an unpleasant experience because the other person did not handle it skillfully. When you have confronted others in the past, it was probably unpleasant because you had no training in what to do and the other person probably responded negatively and defensively.

It is possible for confrontation to be respectful and even caring. Confrontation can be appropriate and valuable for the person being confronted. How can someone improve and change behaviors that affect others negatively if no one will let them know that they are doing something that is a problem?

One of the greatest challenges with behavior problems is learning to identify the behavior rather than judging the person or assuming that you know the reasons for the behavior. To help you gain skill with this important aspect of dealing with problem situations, complete the following exercise.

Labels and Behavior Exercise

With each situation first write in the "label" that someone might use to describe the person, and then figure out how to describe the observable behavior more factually.

1. Sally remarks to Perry, "Where *do* you buy your clothes? I haven't seen an outfit like that since the circus was in town!"

    What label describes Sally? _____

    What is her actual behavior? _____

    _____

2. For the fourth time this month, Jeremy's expense report is incomplete and contains several computational errors.

    What label describes Jeremy? _____

    What is his actual behavior? _____

    _____

3. Wilbur has just swatted Ann on her buttocks with a rolled-up magazine and said, "I sure like the way that skirt fits!"

    What label describes Wilbur? _____

    What is his actual behavior? _____

    _____

4. Monica is shouting angrily at three of her employees, "Why can't you morons learn how to do this right? If you don't get your production figures up with the other team's, you're going to get yourselves fired!"

    What label describes Monica? _____

    What is her actual behavior? _____

    _____

COMPARE YOUR ANSWERS

The labels come easily don't they? Learning to stop judging and attaching negative labels is an important step toward self-empowerment. The self-empowered person makes the extra effort to withhold judgment and to discuss problems with others in a way that communicates respect, even when their behavior is such that most people would disapprove of it.

Compare your answers with those of the authors.

1. Sally could be described as a snob or hateful or tacky.

   Her actual behavior is making a disparaging remark about Perry's clothing.

2. Jeremy could be described as sloppy, careless or lazy.

   His actual behavior is submitting reports with omissions and computational errors.

3. Wilbur could be described as a flirt, a male chauvinist pig, or as obnoxious, fresh or gross.

   His actual behavior is swatting Ann's buttocks and making a sexually suggestive remark. Describing it as sexual harassment would be accurate, but not as helpful as our more specific description in a confrontation discussion.

4. Monica could be described as dictatorial, bossy or insensitive toward others.

   Her actual behavior is shouting at employees and threatening them.

FOUR STEPS TO PREPARE FOR CONFRONTATION

To effectively resolve problems such as these and the one you were thinking about earlier, learn to write down answers to the following four steps.

1. **Define the behavior.** Identify what the person does that you wish they did not do or what they do not do that you wish they would do. Define what they do that you wish they would do differently. Avoid using judgmental or accusatory words when you describe the behavior. Use a factual, nonblaming description in order to reduce defensive reactions.

Example: Arriving for work after 8:00, staying on break more than 15 minutes, telling customers they should have followed instructions.

Practice: Describe the behavior of the person in the problem situation you described on page 86. If you used labels earlier, simply describe the observed behavior that led you to attach that label.

_____

_____

_____

2. **Impact of the behavior.** How does the other person's behavior create a measurable negative impact? What does it cost? Money? Time? Productivity? There may be several undesirable tangible effects that could result from their behavior. Identify these possible results, because you may want to explain one or two of them during your discussion.

Example: Others may follow the example, others may feel angry or resentful, which will affect their productivity, the customer may buy elsewhere.

Practice: Identify at least two or three ways that the behavior of the other person has had an undesirable impact or could have if the behavior continues. It is usually a good idea to list several possibilities to increase the likelihood that you will find one that will impress the other person as a good reason to change their behavior.

_____

_____

_____

FOUR STEPS TO PREPARE
FOR CONFRONTATION (continued)

3. **Your emotions.** You are very likely to have an emotional response when someone's behavior affects you negatively. If you do not express these feelings, they accumulate, which can result in your exploding inappropriately sometime later or at someone else who doesn't deserve your attack. If you store up too many unexpressed emotions, you can even create health problems. To help you identify the negative feelings involved, consider the major categories: *mad, sad,* and *scared.*

Example: *Concerned* that others will follow the example, *worried* that others' resentment will affect productivity, and *afraid* that the customer will not return. You might also be *disappointed* or *angry.*

Practice: Identify your feelings in the problem situation you have been describing. You may want to note the feeling you have about each negative effect.

_____

_____

_____

4. **Your objective.** What do you hope to accomplish with your confrontation? Do you want the person to stop the behavior in question or to use a different behavior? Are you willing to have them suggest alternatives? We recommend asking *them* for a solution because we have found that most people are more likely to remember a commitment and make sure they really follow through when it was something they thought of themselves. We also suggest *asking* for what you want rather than using a *command,* which may sound too intimidating and interfere with a successful negotiation outcome.

Example: Will you please be at work by 8:00? Will you please limit your breaks to 15 minutes? What do you think would be a more effective approach to use with customers who complain about how the product works?

Practice: List one or more outcomes that would satisfy you in solving the problem. You may want to consider several to increase the chances of a win–win compromise. Be sure to consider asking the other person for their solution.

_____

_____

_____

PLAN WHAT YOU WILL SAY

The answers to these four items will help you prepare for the confrontation discussion. The next step is to plan what you will say. It is a good idea to write out some possible openings and other statements you intend to make during the discussion. You may also want to rehearse the statements until you can say them in a respectful, nonthreatening manner. Mental rehearsal of the whole discussion helps to assure a successful negotiation. Remember to imagine positive pictures.

How will it sound? The following examples will help.

Perry could say to Sally, ''Sally, I feel hurt and embarrassed when you make remarks about my clothes, particularly when you do it in front of others. Will you please not make such comments in the future?''

You might say to Jeremy, ''Jeremy, several of your expense reports have been incomplete and contained some errors. This results in my assistant taking time from other duties to contact you for the missing information and to correct your mistakes. I'm annoyed that his time is being used this way. Will you please be sure that your reports are complete and accurate?''

Ann could confront Wilbur with, ''Wilbur, I strongly dislike your hitting me and your remark about my skirt was inappropriate. Will you please apologize and never do that again?''

Wilbur's manager could confront Wilbur because his behavior could harm the manager and the organization if Ann files a sexual harassment charge. The manager might say, ''Wilbur, I saw you swat Ann with your magazine and I heard you make a remark about the way her clothes fit. I'm disappointed that you did that and concerned that Ann might charge sexual harassment if you do something like that again. Will you please make sure that your interaction with her is professional from now on?''

Monica's employees could confront her by saying, ''When you yell at us and threaten to fire us, we feel embarrassed and angry. We are concerned about maintaining a good relationship with you and request that you give us performance feedback in a more helpful manner.''

Monica's manager would also have a right to confront her because her behavior could affect productivity, turnover, etc. The manager could say, ''Monica, I'm concerned about how you handled that situation with your employees just now. Shouting and using threats may result in resentment and rebellion rather than improvement. What do you suggest as a better way to deal with those three?''

PLAN WHAT YOU WILL SAY (continued)

It sounds easy when we provide the words, doesn't it? You can learn to confront appropriately and effectively too, but it will require some practice. Just preparing your answers to the four questions before the confrontation is not enough. Your skill will only develop with practice.

We suggest that you complete your preparation for the problem situation you have used for practice and have a discussion with the person soon. Only by actually doing it will you ever gain self-confidence and skill. When you do, you will have become significantly more self-empowered. Write below what you will say to the other person.

_____

_____

_____

At this point you might ask, "But what happens when I try this and the other person gets angry or starts crying or something like that?" You are quite right that a defensive response is a good possibility. People are not accustomed to being confronted appropriately and they may react emotionally. When someone becomes emotional they may cry, attack you angrily, deny their behavior, or make phony excuses. What do you do when you hear someone being emotional? _____

If you answered, "Restate their feelings and some content," congratulations! The best way to defuse their defensive response is to use your listening feedback skills. You may need to restate their words and acknowledge their feelings a number of times before they calm down, but eventually they will. When they do, continue the discussion by saying somthing else. You have the advantage of being prepared and skillful when you have practiced both sets of skills—confrontation and listening. What a sense of self-empowerment and what a way to empower others by helping to negotiate a real win–win agreement!

In this section we have presented some ideas about how to improve your management skills in delegating responsibilities, coaching people who have made mistakes, and confronting problem behavior.*

* For more help with these and other management skills, we recommend these books from the list at the back of this book: _Delegating for Results_ by Robert Maddux; _Managing Disagreement Constructively_ by Herbert Kindler; _Personal Performance Contracts_ by Roger Fritz; _Team Building_ by Robert Maddux; _An Honest Day's Work_ by Twyla Dell; _Giving and Receiving Criticism_ by Patti Hathaway; and _Practical Time Management_ by Marion Haynes.

S E C T I O N

6

A Personal
Development Program

A PERSONAL DEVELOPMENT PROGRAM

Becoming fully self-empowered takes time and practice. Now that you know how to build your self-esteem, how to change some of your expectations and attitudes, and how to improve your interpersonal and management skills, you need to plan a continuing program for growth and development. Reading this book and completing the exercises will not transform you, but you *can* make significant changes by continuing to use what you have learned.

One of the benefits of being a self-empowered person is that you can have more of what you want from life. An important first step in using your self-empowered abilities is to clarify your values and priorities. To clarify what you intend to accomplish in your personal development program, complete the following exercise.

Identifying Values and Priorities

One of the unique characteristics of each person is his or her value system, and this is part of what makes motivation such a challenge. Knowing your own values and priorities is very important for your personal growth and success. Identify your values in each of the areas explained below.

► **Work.** What is important to you with respect to work? Do you value challenge, interesting work, recognition, involvement, power or control, self-expression or creativity, low stress? List all the work-related factors that are important to you.

_____   _____   _____

_____   _____   _____

_____   _____   _____

► **Relationships.** What are your values with respect to other people? Do you value having a loving family, many close friends or a few, close relationships at work? Is it important for you to have relationships that involve love, trust, honesty, sexuality, sharing, companionship? List all your relationship values.

_____   _____   _____

_____   _____   _____

_____   _____   _____

IDENTIFYING VALUES AND PRIORITIES (continued)

► **Financial.** What is important to you about finances? Do you value owning nice things, having extra money for travel, being financially secure and debt-free for your retirement years, or being wealthy with "money to burn"? List all your values related to finances.

_____   _____   _____

_____   _____   _____

_____   _____   _____

► **Living.** What do you value about living in general? Do you value health and physical fitness, recreation and play, arts, theater or other forms of entertainment, reading, learning, creativity, spirtuality or religion, helping others, protecting the environment? List your general living values.

_____   _____   _____

_____   _____   _____

_____   _____   _____

► **Other values.** What else is important to you? Do you want fame, to be remembered after you are gone, to contribute something that will benefit everyone, to see the world, to own your own business, to travel in space, or something else we have not considered? List all your other values.

_____   _____   _____

_____   _____   _____

_____   _____   _____

Now count the values you listed in all of the categories. Divide the total by 3 and write the number here _____ .

Establishing Priorities

One of the harsh realities of life is that you cannot have it all. Although you can certainly enjoy great success and achieve most of your goals, the likelihood of having *all* of your values satisfied is small. To satisfy your most important values, it is a good idea to establish priorities.

Now you will assign priorities—High, Moderate, or Low—to each of your listed values. However, to be realistic, assign only one-third of your values (the number you wrote in the space on page 98) to each of the three categories. Here is what each category means:

A = **Highest priority.** These are the values that are most important to you. You may already have them in your life or you may be working to achieve them, but you value them very much.

B = **Moderate priority.** These values are important to you but less so than the A values. You would be more comfortable giving up one of these than one of the A values.

C = **Lowest priority.** These are the ones you value the least. You might like to have these in your life, but you are most willing to sacrifice these values in order to have your A and B values satisfied.

Write one of these priority letters beside each of the values you identified in the earlier exercise, but remember to put only one-third of them into each category.

Some of those choices are not easy, but it is important for the rest of your personal development program to have a clear picture of your values and priorities. The next step is to define some goals or objectives that will help you design your life to be consistent with your value priorities. Your life will be satisfying to the degree that what you do is consistent with your values.

DEFINE YOUR GOALS

DEFINE YOUR GOALS

A goal is a statement of what you intend to accomplish. It is an end result, an achievement. A goal is the reason for doing what you do; it is not a task. Tasks are actions taken to meet goals. Many people make lists of things to do, and they may do everything on their lists but still feel like their lives are empty because they have not clarified their values and set appropriate goals. They are people who do a lot, but gain little satisfaction from their accomplishments.

Self-empowered people not only accomplish most of what they set out to do but they also have a clear idea of *why* they are doing what they do, and this helps them enjoy great satisfaction from what they accomplish. If your career *value* is achievement and promotion, your *goals* might include completing a business degree or learning more about the opportunities within your organization. If your *value* is a good marriage, your *goals* might include completing some psychotherapy or counseling or participating in a workshop for couples.

When you define your goals, you can assure success if you make sure that your goals fit the following six criteria:

SIMPLE AND SPECIFIC. Goals need to be clearly understood and easy to remember. A vague goal is unlikely to be accomplished. A complex goal needs to be broken down into simpler goals to ensure success.

MEASURABLE. The only way to know whether you have accomplished your goal is if you have some way to measure it. Ideally you can use numbers to evaluate your progress and achievement.

ATTAINABLE. An impossible goal guarantees failure. To assure success, make your goals realistic and achievable.

RESULTS. State goals in terms of the expected outcome. This helps prevent your defining tasks or steps without clearly identifying what you intend to achieve.

TIME LIMIT. Without a deadline or time limit it is too easy to procrastinate. A time limit helps you stay focused on your goal. A long-term goal may need to be broken down into several shorter-term goals.

SHARED. Few of our achievements are solo performances. You increase your chances for success when you share your goals with others who can support your efforts. Another reason for telling others what you intend to accomplish is that you increase your level of commitment when you make your goals known to others.

PRACTICE GOALS

As you may have noticed, the goal criteria can be remembered with the acronym SMARTS. It is very smart to know your values and plan to have those values satisfied by setting goals related to each. This takes quite a bit of time to do, but it is an investment of time that will pay the dividends of success and self-empowerment.

Invest whatever amount of time is required to define goals for all of your higher priority values. You may have several goals related to one value. Get a little experience with this process right now by choosing a few of your values and writing at least one goal for each. Later you can do a complete job of setting your personal development goals.

Value: _____

Goal: I will _____

_____

_____

Value: _____

Goal: I will _____

_____

_____

Value: _____

Goal: I will _____

_____

_____

Now take a few more minutes to check your goals against the SMARTS criteria. Because most of us have not been taught about setting goals, it is easy to leave something out. By making sure each goal passes the SMARTS test, you are adding to your self-empowerment by increasing your chances for success.

Here is an amazing experience you will probably have: you will accomplish many of your goals without having a definite plan. Once you have a quality goal clearly defined and embedded in your subconscious, you tend to go about achieving it without even being aware that you are doing so. Self-empowered people don't count on this happening, though, and the next step in your personal development program is to design action steps for each goal.

BRAINSTORMING

Sharing your goals is a very good idea because you can call upon the experience and creativity of others to help you develop your action plans. Research in problem solving has shown that the old saying "Two heads are better than one" is true. A brainstorming session in which two or more people combine ideas produces many more quality ideas than any one person could generate alone.

To do brainstorming with someone else, establish two rules in advance: (1) Anything goes—all ideas will be accepted and written down. (2) No criticism—hold evaluation of the ideas until later and do not make negative comments about any idea no matter how weird it might be. These rules free up creativity and keep the ideas coming.

ACTION STEPS

For each of the goals you have defined, list several action steps that will lead to the accomplishment of your goal. Anything that will contribute to the eventual accomplishment can be listed here. Later you can decide which actions you will actually take and in what order you will complete the tasks.

Example:

Value: health and physical fitness.

Goal: I will lose ten pounds during the next 90 days and will maintain my weight at this new level.

Action steps: Read a book on nutrition and exercise, join a health club, exercise three or four days each week for a minimum of 30 minutes each time, switch from ice cream to nonfat frozen yogurt, eat smaller quantities, drink 8 glasses of water each day.

GOAL #1 — ACTION STEPS

_____   _____

_____   _____

_____   _____

_____   _____

GOAL #2 — ACTION STEPS

_____   _____

_____   _____

_____   _____

_____   _____

GOAL #3 — ACTION STEPS

_____   _____

_____   _____

_____   _____

_____   _____

We encourage you to invest the time to develop action steps for each of your goals to help ensure that you live your life in a way that is consistent with the values you have identified as being most important to you. This is the best way to guarantee success in all aspects of your life.

Another tip that will help you accomplish your goals is to put time limits on each of the action steps you choose for the goal. Procrastination is a common problem with goal achievement and time limits help to keep you on track.

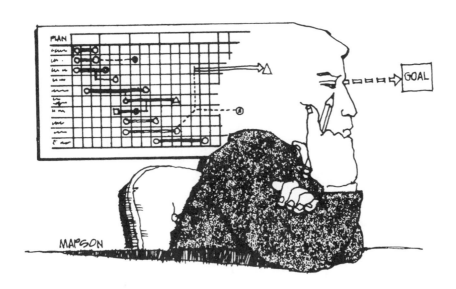

CREATING SUPPORT SYSTEMS

It can make a big difference in your personal development program to arrange a support system for yourself. Self-empowered people know that they do not have to accomplish everything alone and that involving others in their lives adds to their enjoyment and empowers them.

What do we mean by a support system? We are referring to those people who help you, who encourage you, who listen to your concerns and troubles, who provide information, who hold you and comfort you, who play with you, and who help you celebrate your successes. It will help you carry out your personal development program to identify these people, share your goals with them, and involve them in developing your plans for accomplishment.

My Support Group

Identify who gives you the following types of support, and consider how well they do it. We suggest rating them from 1 (poor) to 5 (excellent). You may have more than one person in some categories or you may have none. Think about who else might provide this support for you if your current person does not do it to your satisfaction or if you have no one for this support.

Support	Person	Rating	Who Else?
Encouragement	_____	_____	_____
Assistance	_____	_____	_____
Comfort	_____	_____	_____
Information	_____	_____	_____
Listening	_____	_____	_____
Challenge	_____	_____	_____
Fun/Celebration	_____	_____	_____

If you discovered that you tend to depend upon the same person for all of these types of support, you may want to consider adding more people to your support group. How would you cope if you lost this one person? How much more support could you enjoy if you allowed more people into your life? How much richer could your life become by sharing it with others?

REWARD THE "LITTLE KID" INSIDE YOURSELF

A final suggestion for your personal development program is that you set up a reward system for yourself. The idea of having such a program is to increase the number of successes in your life and to add to the pleasure of having your important values satisfied. Sometimes it will take a long time to reach a goal; and it is easy to become discouraged or to lose sight of the eventual satisfaction waiting for you when you finally achieve your long-term goal. Rewards for completing tasks along the way will keep you going and provide you with more energy for the quest.

Some of the best rewards are those that please the young child who still lives inside you, the little kid who is the primary source of your creativity, enthusiasm, play, intuition and emotions. It is our little kid who is so easily discouraged or disappointed and who needs the revitalization of frequent rewards.

What Does Your "Little Kid" Like?

Check all of the following that appeal to the young child inside you. Be spontaneous and playful as you read the list and allow yourself to check any that appeal to you. (Turn off that disapproving parent who lives in there, too!)

☐ Having a party		☐ Gifts	
☐ New clothes		☐ Playing sports	
☐ Surprises		☐ Records/compact discs	
☐ "Fun food" treats		☐ Going to movies/theater	
☐ Spectator sports		☐ Making love	
☐ Dancing		☐ Comedians	
☐ Travel		☐ Night out with boys/girls	

REWARD THE "LITTLE KID" INSIDE YOURSELF (continued)

Got the idea now? While you are in the mood, list other specific rewards that would motivate you. You can list anything you want!

More Fun Stuff I Like:

_____   _____

_____   _____

_____   _____

Now that you have identified some of the things you would enjoy as rewards for your efforts, make definite plans to give one of these to yourself when you complete an action step or when you achieve a goal within a time limit you set. Ask someone else to give you one of these rewards when they see you doing what you have committed to do or to surprise you with a reward if they notice that you are becoming discouraged. What a wonderful way to involve others in your personal development program and your life. This idea works and will help you achieve your goals!*

* For more help with your personal development program, order the following books from the list at the back of this book: _Comfort Zones_ by Elwood Chapman; _Effective Networking_ by Venda Raye-Johnson; _Personal Wellness_ by Rick Griggs; _Finding Your Purpose_ by Barbara J. Braham; and _Successful Self-Management_ by Paul Timm.

SECTION

7

Maintaining Momentum

MAINTAINING MOMENTUM

We have said repeatedly throughout this book that you will need to practice and use the ideas if you are going to become a self-empowered person. Adult educators tell us that within 24 hours you will forget up to 75 percent of what you learned today, and two weeks from now you will have forgotten 90 percent. The human memory greatly resembles a sieve!

In this final chapter we offer some suggestions to help you remember what you have learned and to help you continue with your movement toward self-empowerment.

First of all, review this book tomorrow. If you do this one simple thing, you will be more likely to remember about 75 percent of what you learned. Unless you have a photographic memory, you are going to forget some of it, but a review within 24 hours will help you retain much more. Read it again within two weeks and think about your answers to the exercises, change some if they need to be changed, write new goals as you think of them. This second review will keep your retention high.

Another way to set these lessons more firmly in your memory is to talk with someone about what you learned. The ideas you share with them will be what you will remember best. There is an old saying that tells us, ''The best way to learn something is to teach it,'' and that certainly seems to be true. When you discuss these ideas with others you are recording them in your long-term memory.

In footnotes throughout this book we have suggested other books from Crisp Publications that will add to the lessons in this book. There are other books from other publishers that we recommend as well. This list is at the end of this section. These books can be found in your local library or favorite bookstore. Bookstores are usually willing to order titles they do not have in stock. We suggest that you make a commitment right now to get at least two or three of the Crisp Publications books we have recommended by ordering them from your local distributor, telephoning Crisp Publications to place an order or visiting your library or bookstore within the next week.

MAINTAINING MOMENTUM (continued)

Another delightful way to learn is through audio- and videotape programs. Many of the titles in the Crisp Publications collection have accompanying video and audio programs that you may want to buy or rent to supplement your reading. We have also listed programs from other sources that relate to some of the topics covered in this book.

Personal growth and self-empowerment is much like personal hygiene or exercise: you have to practice the behaviors regularly for a while before they become habit. By using the ideas and techniques regularly (even daily), you will eventually find that you are doing them automatically. Continuing self-empowerment will become a wonderful new habit. We wish you much success!

Momentum Checklist

☐ 24-hour Review   ☐ Take a course or seminar

☐ 1-week Review   ☐ Buy audio/video program

☐ Share ideas   ☐ 1-month review

☐ Buy at least two books ☐ A reward for following up

OTHER RECOMMENDED READING

Personal Growth

Briggs, Dorothy Corkille. *Celebrate Your Self.* Doubleday, 1977.

Butler, Pamela. *Talking to Yourself.* Harper & Row, 1981.

Dyer, Wayne. *Your Erroneous Zones.* Avon, 1976.

James, Muriel. *It's Never Too Late to Be Happy.* Addison-Wesley, 1985.

McKay, Matthew, & Patrick Fanning. *Self-Esteem.* New Harbinger, 1987.

McKay, M., M. Davis, & P. Fanning. *Messages: The Communications Skills Book.* New Harbinger, 1983.

Relationships

Hendrix, Harville. *Getting the Love You Want.* Harper & Row, 1988.

Paul, Jordan, & Margaret Paul. *Do I Have to Give Up Me to Be Loved by You?* Compcare, 1983.

Management Skills

Burley-Allen, Madelyn. *Managing Assertively.* John Wiley & Sons, 1981.

Byham, William. *Zapp! The Lightning of Empowerment.* Harmony Books, 1991.

Gordon, Thomas. *Leader Effectiveness Training.* Peter Wyden, 1971.

LeBoeuf, Michael. *The Greatest Management Principle in the World.* Berkeley, 1986.

Audio Programs

Lloyd, Sam, & Linda Stone. *Win–Win Relationships.* SuccessSystems, Dallas, Texas.

Tracy, Brian. *The Psychology of Achievement.* Nightingale-Conant.

NOTES

NOTES

NOTES

NOTES

NOTES

NOTES

NOTES

NOTES

OVER 150 BOOKS AND 35 VIDEOS AVAILABLE IN THE 50-MINUTE SERIES

We hope you enjoyed this book. If so, we have good news for you. This title is part of the best-selling *50-MINUTE*™ *Series* of books. All *Series* books are similar in size and identical in price. Many are supported with training videos.

To order *50-MINUTE* Books and Videos or request a free catalog, contact your local distributor or Crisp Publications, Inc., 1200 Hamilton Court, Menlo Park, CA 94025. Our toll-free number is (800) 442-7477.

50-Minute Series Books and Videos Subject Areas . . .

Management
Training
Human Resources
Customer Service and Sales Training
Communications
Small Business and Financial Planning
Creativity
Personal Development
Wellness
Adult Literacy and Learning
Career, Retirement and Life Planning

Other titles available from Crisp Publications in these categories

Crisp Computer Series
The Crisp Small Business & Entrepreneurship Series
Quick Read Series
Management
Personal Development
Retirement Planning